Reviews of earlier titles by Mary Jane Walker

'Highly Recommended'

"This person is courageous. To actually leave everything behind, pack up and go. At the same time, to be truthful, I envy her. I'm sure it took planning and skill. Most of all it took all these generous and thoughtful people to be there. At first, I thought this adventure was going to be tedious. Turns out it's different, fascinating and wonderful. This book shows all elements like where you visit, how are the people leading their lives, what is the food like, the hotels or hostels are they secure, is the staff friendly, are the people you meet honest. Overall, I enjoyed this author and am looking forward to reading her again."

Ross Knight, review of A Maverick Traveller, *initial Amazon Kindle edition, 2 February 2017*

'An interesting read!'

"There are a lot of interesting things in New Zealand. Like Mary Jane, I also love to travel and one of my so-called "travel-goals" is New Zealand. I often heard from my friends who have been to the country about how great it is, how fresh the air is in there and how breathtakingly beautiful the country is. In this book, Mary Jane shares her first-hand experience in New Zealand that will surely inspire readers to dream and pursue that dream to see this country. For me, this book is a sort of travel guide. You will [have] a lot of ideas as to what to do whenever [you] get the chance to visit New Zealand. I had a great time reading this book. I felt that I was already travelling there but of course, I will visit the country for real."

Joo Yoo Rin, review of A Maverick New Zealand Way, *initial Amazon Kindle edition, 30 March 2017*

CUBAN WAY

MARY JANE WALKER

Mary Jane Walker is a writer of historically well-informed travel memoirs. She has been described as a younger, female Bill Bryson, though with her own unique voice. *A Maverick Cuban Way* is the third book in a series of eight

Mary Jane always wanted to visit Cuba, an island nation that conjures up images of revolution, romance and roaming back in time.

Being a Maverick, it is just so fitting to go to Cuba, an island which rejected America's way of doing things.

So too did the author's home country New Zealand, in a smaller way: it rejected visits from nuclear-powered submarines (Mary Jane at age 15 kicked one of these) and vessels carrying nuclear weapons and declared itself nuclear free, and was excluded from a military alliance because of it.

She travelled the whole island in three weeks and loved it. She ate in a restaurant that Harry Belafonte was attending; went to the Sierra Maestra Mountains where Fidel hid as a guerrilla for 18 months; and climbed Pico Turquino, the highest peak in Cuba.

She met and spoke with taxi drivers, academics and locals from all over Cuba. Though the country is poor many are happy, and do not want to see a society with a major income divide re-emerge.

Instagram: @a_maverick_traveller
Twitter: @Mavericktravel0
Facebook: www.facebook.com/amavericktraveller
Linkedin: Mary Jane Walker

Other books by Mary Jane Walker

A Maverick Traveller

A Maverick Traveller is a funny, interesting adventure compilation of Mary Jane's adventures until 2016. Starting from her beginnings in travel it follows her through a life filled with travel and exploration of cultures, mountains, histories and more. Whether it was eating dog unintentionally in Indonesia, meeting the rapper 50 Cent at a backpackers' hostel or kicking a US nuclear submarine in New Zealand, A Maverick Traveller is filled with the unique stories and experiences of Mary Jane Walker.

http://a-maverick.com/books/a-maverick-traveller

A Maverick New Zealand Way

Discover the stunning back country of New Zealand. Come along with Mary Jane on over fifty walks and mountain ascents throughout the islands of New Zealand. Offering an interesting account of New Zealand history alongside tales of modern-day adventure, it is the perfect read to inspire you to get outdoors in New Zealand.

http://a-maverick.com/books/new-zealand-way

A Maverick Pilgrim Way   *Release: September 2017*

Follow the winding ancient roads of pilgrims across the continent of Europe. The Camino de Europa traverses nations, mountains and ranges. Mary Jane has dedicated her life to completing it, one section at a time.

http://a-maverick.com/books/pilgrim-way

A Maverick USA Way   *Release: September 2017*

Mary Jane took AMTRAK trains to East Glacier, West Glacier, Tetons, Estes and Yosemite national parks before the snow hit. She loved the Smithsonian museums and after seeing a live dance at the Native Museum, she decided to go to Standing Rock. It was a protest over land rights and drinking water, at 30 below zero! She loved Detroit which is going back to being a park, and Galveston and Birmingham, Alabama. She was there during the election and was not surprised Trump won. She was tired of being mistaken for being a homeless person because she had a back pack and left San Francisco because of it.

http://a-maverick.com/books/USA-way

A Maverick Himalayan Way   *Release: November 2017*

Mary Jane walked for ninety days and nights throughout the Himalayan region and Nepal, a part of the world loaded with adventures and discoveries of culture, the people, their religions and the beautiful landscapes. She visited the Hindu Kush in Pakistan and listened to the Dalai Lama in Sikkim, India. It is a journey of old and new. So, come trekking in the Himalayas with Mary Jane.

http://a-maverick.com/books/himalayan-way

A Maverick Inuit Way and the Vikings   *Release: December 2017*

Mary Jane's adventures in the Arctic take her dog sledding in Greenland, exploring glaciers and icebergs in Iceland, and meeting some interesting locals. She found herself stuck on a ship in the freezing Arctic Ocean amongst icebergs, and had her car windows almost blown out by gale force winds! Take a ride through the Arctic and its fascinating history.

http://a-maverick.com/books/inuit-way

Plus: *A Maverick Australian Way*, due out in January 2018

Image and Font Acknowledgements

Cover Images

The image of Cuba from space is artwork incorporating architectural distortion to produce a mild oblique effect and removal or blurring of some oceanic cloud cover for clarity. It is based on an image called 'Cuba-MERIS, 28 February 2003' uploaded by the European Space Agency (ESA).

The image of the red car in a concrete-lined street is cropped from a public domain (CC0) image dated 26 March 2016 with keywords Cuba, Havana, Oldtimer, Car, Auto, Red, Street, and Urban (on Pixabay).

The main image on the back cover is a view of the Viñales Valley, consisting of cropped detail from a larger public domain image by Alfredo Avila dated 10 October 2007 (in Wikimedia Commons).

Colours, brightness and contrast have been deepened and intensified in all cover images as needed in order to make image and/or lettering stand out.

Fonts

The interior of the print version of this book was typeset in Adobe Garamond Pro using Adobe InDesign. The front cover and spine were typeset in League Gothic, in bold capitals for the title and normal text for the author's name. The back cover was typeset in Handlee (regular), made bold using Microsoft Publisher.

Interior Images

Where images used in the interior are not the property of the author, their sources are acknowledged in the relevant captions. Interior images have also been brightened and/or intensified in some cases. Where more significant alterations have been made, such as architectural perspective correction and/or cropping, these have been noted in the image caption if the image is not the property of the author.

All maps and aerial views are credited with the original source, and have north at the top unless indicated otherwise.

All photographs in the book are the property of Mary Jane Walker unless otherwise acknowledged

ISBN-13: 978-0-473-40833-6

Disclaimer

This book is a travel memoir, not an outdoors guide. Although the author and publisher have made every effort to ensure that the information in this book was correct at the time of publication, the author and publisher do not assume and hereby disclaim any liability to any party for any loss, damage, or disruption caused by errors or omissions, whether such errors or omissions result from negligence, accident, or any other cause. Some names may also have been changed to disguise and protect certain individuals.

Contents

Introduction

C UBA is the Cinderella of the world, yet to realise its true worth. It's raggedy with a heart of gold, but at times glitters and has gold dust and rich carriages in the form of classic cars in bright colours. It is not a Western society. Expect the unexpected and it will happen. Batteries in the clockwork of time have stopped and it is like going back to the 1950s both in the cars, and in the shops.

Cuba is the sort of place I am drawn to. Why? Because I think you can make a distinction between travellers and tourists, and I consider myself within the first group. I like to go to the places less visited. There

The Plaza Vieja in Havana is worth wandering around for a refreshing taste of renovated Spanish colonial architecture.

is something about places that are just a little bit off the beaten track that gets the blood pumping and my heart racing with excitement and pure joy.

I love cultures, I love people, and I love getting to know them. The people in the hostels I stay at are more than just the 'staff' – they are mothers, wives, husbands, fathers and grandmothers, and everyone has their story. I have been travelling for a long time, my passion for travel ignited by my first overseas trip to Scotland to catch up with family.

Ever since, you will have found me somewhere different, and I have a long list of destinations planned. In fact, it is completely normal for me to be somewhere overseas and already planning my next trip. I have a penchant for travelling. Travel is my true passion, my love.

Cuba has always been of interest to me. I've heard other people describe it as laid-back, old-fashioned and hectic all at once. An island sitting amongst the rolling blue of the Caribbean, beautiful and complex, marked by history. And so, I had to go there.

Though I saw a lot and did more research for this book when I got home, I feel I've only scratched the surface. One thing is for sure: I'll be back!

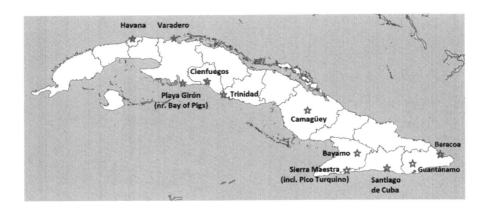

Places I visited in Cuba. Map background by NordNordWest in Wikimedia Commons, CC-BY- SA 3.0.

CHAPTER ONE
A Slice of Cuban History

J ust over eleven million people inhabit Cuba. And four million tourists now visit Cuba annually, a number massively up from the mere quarter of a million of a generation or so back, in the mid-1980s.

The history of Cuba is very complex, so I will only briefly touch on it here. It is a mixture of colonialism and conquest, with a touch of pirate in places.

Well before Fidel Castro and the Cuban revolution, Christopher Columbus created the first European settlement in the Americas on a large island south-east of Cuba occupied today by Haiti and the Dominican Republic. Columbus named this island la Isla Española, the Spanish Island. It is known today in English as Hispaniola.

There were already people living on Hispaniola and nearby islands, including Cuba. The most numerous of these and the chief occupiers of the larger islands of the Caribbean were the Taíno, originally from South America. The Taíno are thought to have known Hispaniola by a name spelt Quisqueya in Spanish or Kiskeya in Haitian Creole. The name is said to have meant 'mother of all lands', 'big island' or 'proliferating earth', as Hispaniola was large, mountainous and the centre of an expanding Taíno realm at the time of the Spanish conquest. The name of Cuba also comes from a word of Taíno origin, meaning something like 'abundant land'.

On the smaller islands of the Caribbean there lived the Carib, another Amerindian people. The Carib gave their name to the Caribbean. And there was a third indigenous people living at the extreme western end of Cuba at the time of the Spanish conquest. These were called the Guanahatabey or Guanahacabibes.

Then came slavery. The Spanish brought with them African slaves to work on the sugar cane and plantations in Cuba and other islands of the Caribbean.

During the seventeenth century, there came the time of the Caribbean Pirates. Encircling the area like sharks they raided ships and were banished to live life at sea and in little enclaves where they could pull ashore unnoticed.

The wind batters a portrait of Fidel Castro, a portrait that was hanging on the exteriors of many buildings and homes in Havana just after his death.

The building to the right is the headquarters of the Young Communists' League. It sports more permanent portraits, in metal, of revolutionary heroes Julio Antonio Mella (d.1929), Camilo Cienfuegos (d. 1959, with hat), and Ernesto 'Che' Guevara (d. 1967).

4

It sounded fascinating reading about it all at the museums, with notable characters like Blackbeard, Henry Morgan and Bartholomew Roberts appearing and disappearing around the islands of the region.

The first University in Cuba was founded in 1728 in Havana. I don't know what was more amazing: that it was founded so far back, or that Cuba had already been a Spanish colony for more than two hundred years by that time. Castro studied at University to become a lawyer, which I thought was remarkable in view of his subsequent rebel career. Was the courtroom where he got a gift for making speeches? I wonder.

Several European countries wanted to control parts of the Caribbean. There were wars and conquests from Spain, France, Netherlands, and Britain to name but a few, who all fought with each other over Cuba and its neighbouring islands. Cuba was even controlled by the British for a while in 1762, but they gave it back to Spain. Otherwise, the Cubans would be dominating the West Indies line-up on the cricket pitch, I have no doubt.

Cuba's Strategic Location in relation to the Gulf of Mexico, the Caribbean and the Panamà Canal. Map Data ©2017 Google, INEGI

Cuba eventually gained its independence in 1898 following US intervention at the end of a thirty-year struggle for independence punctuated with intervals of peace. The Cubans like to claim that the intervention was not necessary. But the Americans intervened anyway. Part of the reason why was that Cuba is so strategic. The narrow straits that separated Cuba from Mexico's Yucatán peninsula and Florida are obvious choke-points, as is the Windward Passage between Cuba and Hispaniola.

Whoever controlled Cuba was in a good position to control the Gulf of Mexico and the Caribbean. Even before missiles were invented, the potential was there for what the Victorians might have called the Cuban Steamboat Crisis.

The Americans were so concerned about a Cuban blockade that they would build a canal halfway across the middle of Florida. Cuba's Spanish rulers also had a plan to build a canal that *they* could control through the middle of Cuba!

Somewhat ironically in view of its later propensity for revolution, Cuba was known in the first half of the nineteenth century as the 'ever-faithful isle'. It had not significantly taken part in the rebellions by which many other Latin American countries, from Mexico to Chile and Argentina, had become independent in the time of Napoleon.

The present-day Cuban national flag was designed in New York in 1849 by the exiles Narciso López and Migel Teurbe Tolón, who finalised it in consultation with some of the other exiles.

One of the ironies of the design of the Cuban national flag, at least as viewed in the light of subsequent history, is that López had not sought independence from Spain but rather the accession of Cuba into the United States of America, which in 1849 had just taken over Texas, New Mexico, Arizona, Nevada and California from Mexico. What is now the flag of

Cuba was intended to be the flag of a future U. S. state to be carved out of the contested remnants of the Spanish empire, precisely akin to Texas or California. Originally from Venezuela, López, who wasn't even Cuban, ran his flag up on Cuban soil for the first time in 1850 in a short-lived occupation of a northern Cuban town by a boatload of US-financed rebels, of which precisely nothing came at the time, as the island was still faithful to Spain.

Cuba's thirty years of more serious independence wars began in 1868, initially under the direction of a man from the vicinity of the south-eastern city of Santiago de Cuba named Carlos Manuel de Céspedes. De Céspedes favoured another flag which was like the flag of Chile but with the blue and the red reversed. This flag is also quite frequently used in an official capacity and is called the Demajagua or the Yara flag, after the town of Yara near Bayamo where the independence struggles of 1868 began. In 1869 the independence movement adopted López's flag, however.

De Céspedes's flag survives as the flag of government institutions, most obviously as the Cuban Naval Jack, and also hangs in the Cuban parliament alongside the national flag. One thing that is distinctive about Cuba is that present regime draws its legitimacy from earlier independence struggles and has not sought to overturn the old names or their symbols in

Cuban Flags.

This historical image is cropped from a larger one with Spanish text which appears in the blog The Cuba Bug ('In the Museum of the Captain General', 6 February 2015).

7

most cases. The national coat of arms, for instance, was not changed to look more 'Communist' after the Castroites took over. It is just the same as it was when Cuba became independent of Spain at the dawn of the twentieth century.

The last stage of the nineteenth-century independence wars ran from 1895 until 1898. It was inspired and led, at first, by the writer and idealist José Martí, who is probably the only one of Cuba's nineteenth-century revolutionaries to be particularly well known outside of Cuba itself.

Both de Céspedes and Martí were killed in battle in their respective wars. A more fortunate survivor of these conflicts, one who saw action right through from the 1860s, was a General Calixto García.

From 1873 onward, García sported a distinctive dent in his skull caused by the fact that, at the end of a losing battle, he shot himself in the head with a 45-calibre pistol rather than be taken alive. Miraculously, García survived with no disability apart from a tendency to be afflicted by headaches. Granted a second chance at life, he continued the fight for another twenty-five years. Cuban history seems to abound with such individuals.

A billboard with an image of nineteenth century patriot José Martí, stating "the country is made by the merit of its sons/children."

It is short for a sentence that reads, 'The country is made by the merit of its children and its wealth is counted by the wellbeing of your child.'

Most of the fighting in the Cuban theatre of the Spanish-American War of 1898, the American intervention by which Cuba finally won its independence from Spain, took place around the south-eastern

8

*Calixto García (the man in front of the hut in tall boots), US Brigadier
-General William Ludlow (holding hat), and Cuban rebels, 1898.*

This image comes from Harper's Pictorial History of he War with Spain (1899) via
the US Library of Congress, https://www.loc.gov/rr/hispanic/1898/ludlow.html

city of Santiago de Cuba. This fighting included a naval battle offshore and
the famous charge of Theodore Roosevelt's Rough Riders up San Juan Hill.

(In spite of their name, the Rough Riders served on foot throughout the
brief war. They had to leave their horses behind due to lack of shipping,
and ran up not just one but two hills outside Santiago on foot, suffering
heavy losses.)

'Some Time in the Future'.

'When Insurgent and Spaniard have worn themselves out fighting for Cuba,
Uncle Sam may step in and comfort the fair damsel' Puck, *10 July 1985,
cartoonist Louis Dalrymple, US Library of Congress, control number 2012648643*

García and the rebels under his command cooperated closely with the
Americans in 1898. A photograph published just after the war depicts
García alongside an American brigadier-general named William Ludlow.
Well into the twentieth century, 'a message to García' would be an American
popular idiom for something involving plenty of initiative and unorthodoxy.
Apparently, it still has that meaning among the US military.

There was broad domestic support for US intervention in Cuba, both
from those who wanted to see the independence struggle succeed thanks
to America giving it one final push, and also from those who *didn't* want to
see Cuba become too independent. Something of the latter agenda comes
through in an American cartoon from 1895 called "Some Time in the

LA FATLERA DEL ONCLE SAM (per M. MOLINÉ).

Guardarse l' isla perque no 's perdi.

'*The Craving of Uncle Sam*'

Saving the island so it won't get lost' A wrecked boat and swimmers in the water are probably a reference to arms smugglers from the USA ('filibusters'). *Cartoon by Manuel Moliné I Muns, in the Catalan-language periodical* La Campana de Gràcia, *1896. This version from Wikimedia Commons, public domain.*

Future," in which Uncle Sam comforts an allegorical figure of Cuba while the Spanish and the independence fighters exhaust each other.

The same sentiment comes through in an amusing Catalan (*i.e.*, Spanish) cartoon from 1896 called La Fatlera del Oncle Sam, 'The Craving of Uncle Sam', which represents Uncle Sam as a pop-eyed addict whose drug of choice is territorial expansion.

In the Spanish cartoon, you can see a wrecked boat and swimmers in the water. This probably refer to the content of the story 'A foundered filibuster', *Los Angeles Herald*, 29 January 1896. The unseaworthy steamer *J. W. Hawkins* sprang a leak soon after leaving a US port in January 1896 with dozens of would-be guerrillas bound for Cuba aboard, and slowly settled

Contemporary sketches of the Spanish surrender to the United States in what is now the Parque Céspedes, Santiago de Cuba, 17 July 1898.

View to the left is where the Santiago de Cuba Town Hall is now. View to the right shows the Cathedral in background. *Artist: William J. Glackens* US Library of Congress reproduction numbers LC-USZC2-501, LC-USZC4-3683

to the bottom. Boatloads of rebels setting out for Cuba are an old custom, called filibustering in the nineteenth century, a word that comes from a Dutch term for pirate. In the twentieth century, both Castro's supporters, and US-backed rebels at the Bay of Pigs, would carry on the filibustering tradition.

On 17 July 1898, the Spanish surrendered Cuba in the Plaza de Armas in Santiago de Cuba. The Plaza de Armas, the plaza where troops were mustered and where besieged defenders would also gather, was the usual name for the most important square in any town in Spanish America. In Santiago de Cuba this square would later, in our time, be known as Parque Céspedes after the first reasonably successful Cuban freedom fighter, Carlos

Manuel de Céspedes, who was not just Cuban but in fact from Santiago himself. In the meantime, in what was still in 1898 the Plaza de Armas, the surrender was recorded for posterity by the American artist William J. Glackens. Perhaps, as with some courtroom proceedings, it was considered bad form to take pictures.

In a gesture that would curdle relations between the USA and the new nation, the local American commander, Major-General William 'Pecos Bill' Shafter, refused to allow García or any other surviving Cuban independence fighters into Santiago de Cuba – Cuba's second city and a cradle of revolutionists – to take part in the ceremony. The grounds given were that the insurgents might go on a rampage. Not even the officers, such as García, were allowed.

The American war correspondent and novelist Frank Norris wrote the story up in a short book called *The Surrender of Santiago*, which makes no mention of the Cuban fighters other than in passing. Norris claimed no additional help in the city's conquest by a new and more Teutonic tribe of conquistadors:

Here we were in the city at last, riding in, hoofs clattering, sabres rattling, saddles creaking, and suddenly a great wave of exultation came over us all. I know the General felt it. I know the last trooper of the escort felt it. There was no thought of humanitarian principles then. The war was not a "crusade," we were not fighting for Cubans just then, it was not for disinterested motives that we were there sabred and revolvered and carbined. Santiago was ours—was ours, ours, by the sword we had acquired, we, Americans, with no one to help—and the Anglo-Saxon blood of us, the blood of the race that has fought its way out of a swamp in Friesland, conquering and conquering and conquering, on to the westward, the race whose blood instinct is the acquiring of land, went galloping through our veins to the beat of our horses' hoofs.

13

'School Begins'

'Uncle Sam *(to his new class in Civilization)* - Now, children, you've got to learn these lessons whether you want to or not! / But just take a look at the class ahead of you, and remember that, that in a little while, you will feel as glad to be here as they are!'

Puck, *25 January 1899, cartoonist Louis Dalrymple, US Library of Congress, control number 2012647459*

Every trooper that day looked down from his saddle upon Cuban and Spanish soldiers as from a throne. Even though not a soldier, it was impossible not to know their feeling, glorying, arrogant, the fine, brutal arrogance of the Anglo-Saxon, and we rode on there at a gallop through the crowded streets of the fallen city, heads high, sabres clattering, a thousand iron hoofs beating out a long roll—triumphant, arrogant conquerors.[1]

Norris's opinions are obviously unacceptable today. But he felt free to write that way for publication in the main stream media of his time. His views were much the same as those that D. W. Griffiths expressed on film,

1   Frank Norris, *The Surrender of Santiago*, San Francisco, Paul Elder & co, 1917, pp. 19-20.

in his then-popular but now-shocking *Birth of a Nation*. We have forgotten how endemic such prejudices – not just racism but actual Aryanism – once were in English-speaking countries, as well as in Germany, at the height of the age of British empire-building and the American conquest of the Wild West.

A similar degree of racism comes through in a post-conquest cartoon by the same cartoonist who drew the 1895 cartoon above, a cartoon which was published in the same magazine. The blackboards are covered in lessons to the effect that self-government is all very well in theory but seldom observed in practice. Even the British Empire is praised for governing its subject populations without the consent of the governed and thereby contributing to the advance of civilisation.

Presumably, subjects other than the American colonists of 1776 were meant by such praise for what used to be known as 'taxation without representation'. And it is not hard to guess where the line is drawn, it is a line of race or colour. In the cartoon the new children are all black, an American black is washing the windows (having presumably proven ineducable despite the teacher's best efforts), and the native American holds a book upside down. A pigtailed Chinese, heir to an ancient civilisation, is knocking to be let into Uncle Sam's classroom. A dusky Inuit or Dene from Alaska sits among the good children, but maybe she is the exception to the rule.

The day after the Spanish surrender in Santiago, García resigned his post as the leader of the Cuban insurgents in protest. Out of the whole of the next 120 years of potential bliss, it turned out that Uncle Sam's honeymoon with his new Cuban bride, to go by one of the cartoons above, had lasted precisely one day.

Things would only go downhill from there. The negotiations over the peace treaty that would formally end the war and put a legal stamp on

*'The House Brand': Early Twentieth Century
cartoon of the Platt Amendment.*

(Widely reproduced, origins obscure)

Cuba's independence, the Treaty of Paris, were conducted entirely by the Americans and the Spanish, without Cuban involvement.

(Later on, in this book, I will show some photographs of what Santiago's historic Parque Céspedes looks like now. The Cuban freedom fighters might not have been allowed in: but the square is named after one of them all the same.)

García died before the year 1898 was out, from a sudden bout of pneumonia contracted while on diplomatic business in the United States, no doubt trying to secure more say in what was happening to his country. Until 1909, Cuba became effectively a US protectorate, with two periods of direct military government by the USA and a brief interval of freedom in between.

Fearing political volatility and the rise of anti-Americanism, the Americans had imposed a range of rather humiliating conditions on Cuba via the so-called Platt Amendment of 1901, named after an American senator of the day, Orville Platt.

The essence of the Platt Amendment was that the Cubans had to maintain balanced budgets, not enter into any treaties that the Americans did not approve of, and hand over Guantánamo, while for their part the Americans reserved the right to intervene militarily in Cuban affairs any time they felt like it. The Platt Amendment was incorporated word-for-word into the constitution of the new Cuban republic, in ways that engendered another

There are signs of the revolution all around Cuba - literally.

The one at the top, depicting Castroite co-revolutionary and eventual wife of Raúl Castro, Vilma Espin, is from a larger photograph by 'Callelinea' on Wikimedia Commons, Public Domain. The other two were taken by me; the one in the middle shows Fidel Castro and Hugo Chávez with the legend 'Our best Friend'

famous cartoon called El Hierro de la Casa, 'The House Brand', a pun that works in Spanish and English alike. President McKinley is shown branding a serf-like Cuban, while Uncle Sam looks on.

Much of Cuba's land was bought up in a few short years by American speculators, under the cover of occupation and a weak national government. By 1905 the occupation government and the fledgling Cuban regime, under US domination, had presided over the sale of most of the country's land to the Americans. Cuba's new rulers had, quite literally, 'sold out'.

The opportunity to right an ancient wrong – to turn Cubans who had toiled for four hundred years on Spanish estates into free peasants and small farmers – was thus passed up by the Americans in favour of their own agribusiness interests. This made some kind of future revolution, directed at American big business, all but inevitable.

The relationship between Cuba and the USA was renegotiated onto a somewhat more outwardly respectful basis in 1934, under what the new US President Franklin D. Roosevelt called the 'good neighbour' policy toward Latin American. Even so, historians seem to agree that the imposition of humiliating terms by the USA, and the ongoing monopolisation of the land by the Americans, produced exactly the sorts of volatility and anti-Americanism the Americans feared.

Such resentments would ultimately come to overshadow the more positive aspects of

Rugged-looking walls rise up out of concrete streets bordered by narrow footpaths.

Cuban-American ties. Most obviously, these positives had included the fact of American aid in the gaining of Cuban independence as a sort of 'last push'. American engineers started work on Havana's famous coastal walkway the Malecón, a word which means 'Quay'. And the Spanish-American War had also created an opportunity for Cuban and American doctors to come together and prove that a certain species of mosquito transmitted the deadly yellow fever, with the implication being that if the mosquitos were controlled, so too would be the fever. This in turn made it possible to build the Panama Canal, in addition to saving countless lives even in Cuba itself. A drop in the usual death rate became noticeable in Havana, where such measures were first put into effect, as early as 1902.

As far as many Cubans were concerned, the positives were outweighed by the negatives, and revenge for national humiliation and plundering would be served cold some sixty years after the immediate gaining of independence, when Fidel Castro imposed a massively anti-American regime upon Cuba, one that would, of necessity, come into more serious conflict with American still when it started taking the land back.

As the Cubans see it, and indeed in reality, they did produce some exceptional independence movements and leaders, the best-known today being Fidel Castro of course. As such, I made it a point to book a trek to Castro's hideout in the Sierra Maestra mountains in the south of Cuba.

My plan to travel to Cuba began to take shape in June of 2016 – winter for us in New Zealand. After studying a Master's Degree in politics at Auckland University, anything political will catch my attention. I was already intending to be in the United States in time to witness the 2016 elections firsthand. I wouldn't call myself a fan of Fidel Castro, but there was something admirable about him, and his country. The idea popped into my head: take a side trip to Cuba! And so, I did.

19

My start to the year 2017 would involve salsa dancing in the streets of Havana, trekking through the stunning jungles thick with heat and mosquitos and riding in cramped buses along the coastline of Cuba. I figured three weeks would be plenty of time to see Cuba. I think anything over two weeks in a country really pushes everything into perspective – you are usually well past the honeymoon "everything is awesome" stage, and start seeing a place for what it really is.

I would travel to Cuba from Miami, in the south of the United States, on the 28th of December and stay until the 18th of January. It was a short and sweet one-hour plane ride across coast and Caribbean, only six months after such flights had resumed directly from the US, thanks to the thaw in relations pursued by President Obama.

I went to the Buena Vista Social Club in Havana, to Varadero Beach and to Cienfuegos, after which I went to the Bay of Pigs (the site of the American CIA attack in 1961), the Sierra Maestra Mountains, the Turquino National Park, and then on to Santiago de Cuba.

CHAPTER TWO

Some Travellers' (and Tourists') Tips

ACCOMMODATION

T HE first question a traveller or tourist asks, is where to stay? Well, in Cuba, hotels can be quite pricey: the ones pitched most obviously at the tourist trade and run by Western chains — hotels that until quite recently were off-limits to the Cubans themselves, not that many Cubans could afford to stay in them anyway — often average around $300-$400 a night!

That's US dollars, by the way. Visitors to Cuba most use the Cuban convertible peso (CUC) pegged to the US dollar which has existed in banknote form since 2006 and which has exchanged at one to one for the US dollar (USD) since 2011, frosty diplomatic relations notwithstanding. Locals use a 'national money' peso (CUP) which is worth about four cents US and takes the form of a different-looking series of banknotes. It's very important to know which kind of peso you have in your pocket or which kind someone gives you in change! Confusingly, all three currencies are denoted by the symbol $.

In this book, I will use the $ sign to refer to a price denominated either in the USD or CUC, not the national money (CUP).

The value of the convertible peso might change in the future. But when I was there and gathering the facts in this book, it was a US dollar in disguise.

The best way to get either form of money is to exchange foreign currency in a bank that handles foreign money (only in the big cities, apparently), or otherwise a Cadeca (**Ca**sa **de Ca**mbio), a Cuban government money exchange found in most cities. US dollars incur a 10 per cent surcharge, and some other countries' currencies a surcharge as well, so it is best to exchange Euros or Canadian dollars at present. While a traveller or tourist will mostly use CUC pesos, it pays to carry a few hundred CUP pesos as well so as to take advantage of inexpensive local food and produce, especially in out-of-the-way places where CUC pesos are less likely to be accepted in the shops. CUP pesos can also be a good way for backpackers to save money on things like food. Apparently, you can eat for a dollar a day in CUP pesos; albeit perhaps at a somewhat greater risk of getting ill from germs to which you have no immunity, and having your holiday spoiled that way.

The most popular alternative to a hotel is the casa particular, or casas particulares in the plural. Casa particular means 'special house', and it is the Cuban term for a bread-and-breakfast or anything similar such as a

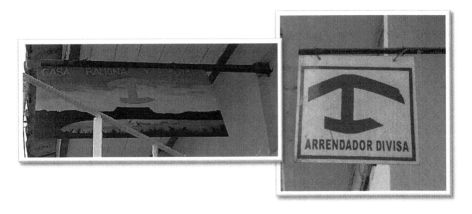

Signs for Casas Particulares Divisa ('divided') is the more formal term for a house with short-stay accommodation. Note the distinctive symbol!

timeshare accommodation where you look after yourself, though it usually means bed-and-breakfast.

Often referred to as casas for short, casas particulares are very much 'what you pay is what you get'. Most casa owners do really look after you well: the only thing is don't expect a hot shower – which is horrible when it is really cold and raining and windy, but that's all part of it I guess. I met a couple who paid $40 a night and they got a hot shower, whereas I was paying $25 and didn't. A lot of casas also make really nice full meals for around $8.

The casas are great: a real authentic way to experience Cuba. But I will warn you – your booking can magically disappear or be cancelled and sold to the highest bidder. That has happened several times to me, and on one such occasion, when I was in Varadero, the lady running it told me she had nothing left. I was fed up and stood my ground and got quite assertive with her so she found me a bed in the lobby.

Although tourist hotels were expensive I found out you can get a room in one much cheaper if you know someone who knows someone who works there, that kind of thing! $38 will get you an awesome room with a great view – but only if you know someone who knows someone! I started to eat at hotels, but I'd always check the kitchens first!

Casas are better booked by phone on the day, so **buy a local sim card** for your phone. Wandering around finding one at whatever hour you find yourself in need of accommodation can get tiring and is the last thing you sometimes want to do.

Talk to the locals, get their recommendations, and talk to other travellers who can also point you in the right direction. Be wary of the peak seasons. January and February are the busiest in the winter months and May and June are the busiest months in the Cuban summer. This is when you will find it harder to book and secure definite accommodation.

A third alternative to the tourist hotels and the casas particulares is to be found in the government-run hotels, which are somewhat more low-key than the tourist hotels and often located in older buildings. I heard of one for about $80 a night that even had a swimming pool. The government-run hotels have a steady provision of water and food and the kitchens are usually well-kept and clean.

The thing is, Cuba is ever changing, going through a metamorphosis into the 21st Century. Once-abandoned and dilapidated buildings are now being pulled down or renovated to make way for some of the bigger international hotel chains and their modern buildings. It is a time of change, so get there sooner rather than later if you want to see the last fragments of Fidel's Cuba.

TRANSPORT

Buses and taxis are the most common modes of transport for travelling between cities Cuba. I drifted between the two and found that sometimes a taxi was better value than a bus. That happened when I went to Guantanamo. It was going to cost me $15 by bus or $20 in a taxi, so I went with the taxi that time.

Or, you could rent a car. But one thing not to do in

Catch a ride back in time in a classic car! Such old-fashioned automobiles, still common in Cuba, were either imported from the USA or assembled by Cuban subsidiaries of American car makers before US trade embargos were imposed in the early 1960s.

CC0 public domain Pixabay image by 'PeterKraayvanger' (retouched).

24

Cuba is to book a rental car online! I had read in my guide books not to bother because the price is ridiculous! Also, I met a New Zealand lady who had booked a rental car online – turned up to collect it and the car and booking were nonexistent. So, don't book a rental car online: there are some hoaxes going on around those, I think. I did try and book a rental car for $100 a day but I couldn't get confirmation of booking. Luckily no money changed hands and I just stuck with the other options.

Talking to other tourists and locals, they all recommended that you book your rental car while you are in the country and not before. That way you don't end up paying over the odds for something that you can't be sure of. The buses between cities seem to run every couple of hours, so there are plenty of opportunities to book one – which can be done online on their website.

BUS TIMETABLES

Don't expect any fancy signs in the stations or at the bus stop. most are handwritten and can get a bit confusing, but here are some rough guides on what to expect and distances between major cities.

Buses were super-cheap, although the process for booking one was a challenge.

PRECIOS PRICES		
DESTINO/DESTINATION	ADULTOS/ADULTS	NIÑOS/CHILDREN
LA HABANA - VARADERO	$ 10,00	$ 5,00
LA HABANA - MATANZAS	$ 7,00	$ 5,00
LA HABANA - TRINIDAD	$ 25,00	$ 12,50
LA HABANA - CIENFUEGOS	$ 20,00	$ 10,00
LA HABANA - ENT. DE JAGÜEY	$ 12,00	$ 6,00
LA HABANA - VIÑALES	$ 12,00	$ 6,00
LA HABANA - LAS TERRAZAS	$ 6,00	$ 5,00
LA HABANA - PINAR DEL RÍO	$ 11,00	$ 5,50
LA HABANA - SANTA CLARA	$ 18,00	$ 9,00
LA HABANA - SANCTI SPÍRITUS	$ 23,00	$ 11,50
LA HABANA - CIEGO DE ÁVILA	$ 27,00	$ 13,50
LA HABANA - CAMAGÜEY	$ 33,00	$ 16,50
LA HABANA - LAS TUNAS	$ 39,00	$ 19,50
LA HABANA - HOLGUÍN	$ 44,00	$ 22,00
LA HABANA - BAYAMO	$ 44,00	$ 22,00
LA HABANA - SANTIAGO DE CUBA	$ 51,00	$ 25,50
SANTIAGO DE CUBA - VARADERO	$ 49,00	$ 24,50
VARADERO - SANTIAGO DE CUBA	$ 49,00	$ 24,50
TRINIDAD - VARADERO	$ 20,00	$ 10,00
VARADERO - TRINIDAD	$ 20,00	$ 10,00
VIÑALES - TRINIDAD	$ 37,00	$ 18,50
SANTIAGO DE CUBA - GUANTÁNAMO	$ 6,00	$ 5,00
TRINIDAD - SANTIAGO DE CUBA	$ 33,00	$ 16,50
SANTIAGO DE CUBA - TRINIDAD	$ 33,00	$ 16,50
SANTIAGO DE CUBA - BARACOA	$ 15,00	$ 7,70

Pricing for Bus Trips. These are CUC peso rates for travelling on Viazul. Secondary services charge the same price but in CUC for foreigner and CUP for locals.

An example of bus timetable information. It pays to check the day before you are due to ride the bus, as timetables may change.

APPROXIMATE DISTANCES IN KILOMETRES	BAYAMO	CAMAGÜEY	CIENFUEGOS	GUANTÁNAMO	HAVANA	HOLGUÍN	MATANZAS	PINAR DEL RIO	SANTA CLARA	SANTIAGO DE CUBA
BARACOA	313	524	853	116	1051	348	989	1192	793	193
BAYAMO		211	540	197	738	71	676	879	480	120
CAMAGÜEY	211		329	408	527	208	465	668	269	331
CÁRDENAS	628	417	171	825	146	625	56	287	148	748
CIEGO DE ÁVILA	321	110	219	518	397	318	335	538	139	441
CIENFUEGOS	540	329		737	246	537	199	387	61	660
GUANTÁNAMO	197	408	737		935	232	873	1076	677	77
HAVANA	738	527	246	935		735	90	141	258	858
HOLGUÍN	71	208	537	232	735		673	876	477	155
LA FÉ	989	778	497	1186	251	986	341	110	509	1109
LAS TUNAS	82	129	458	279	656	79	594	7979	398	202
MANZANILLO	60	271	600	257	798	131	736	39	540	180
MATANZAS	676	465	199	873	90	673		231	196	796
NUEVITAS	286	75	404	483	602	283	540	743	344	406
PALMA SORIANO	73	284	613	124	811	108	749	952	553	47
PINAR DEL RIO	879	668	387	1076	141	876	231		399	999
SANCTI SPIRITUS	395	184	145	592	343	3924	281	484	85	515
SANTA CLARA	480	269	61	677	258	77	196	399		600
SANTIAGO DE CUBA	120	331	660	77	858	155	796	999	600	
TRINIDAD	468	257	72	665	318	465	271	459	122	588

Travel distances around Cuba

Cuban inter-city bus routes and international airport connections

You have to wait in line to book prior to the bus leaving, and then you go back on the day and pay for it. Be prepared for mass lines and even to the point you might not even be able to get onto the bus because it's too full.

There are two types of buses running between cities and towns in Cuba: comparatively luxurious tourist-type coaches run by firms such as Viazul, which primarily cater to foreign visitors, and then others for locals. The buses for locals usually mean you have to stand; but they go to more rural areas and stop at many more places.

Local buses can be a bit grimy, but it's still much better than getting into an overpriced rental car that breaks down all the time! I ended up on one of these local buses from Cienfuegos

Watch out for Horses and Carts!

27

to Trinidad and I was lucky because there weren't a lot of transport options between the two cities.

(Trinidad, a picturesque Cuban city whose name means 'Trinity', is often called Trinidad de Cuba to distinguish it from numerous other Trinidads in the Spanish-speaking world and southern USA, not to mention Trinidad and Tobago. The same goes for Santiago de Cuba, one of fifty or so Santiagos in the wider Hispanic cultural realm. The word Malecón is not unique to Havana either; many other towns and cities have their Malecóns given that Malecón means Quay, or for that matter, Embankment.)

There are two bus drivers on every bus. They are highly organised in that sense, with each driver taking turns in shifts. Perhaps this is because driving in Cuba takes more attention than in a more Western sort of country with better roads and fewer random pedestrians and livestock (which is another reason not to drive oneself). The buses in general make plenty of stops for food and toilets, called baños. Most bus drivers do speak basic English, which is very handy.

My guide book told me to get on the trains and go around Cuba. When I looked further into the idea, I found that the trains were virtually non-existent. The railway tracks I saw were heavily overgrown with long grass and to be honest didn't look all that safe.

I got a bus from Baracoa to Camagüey inland for $33 and then one from Camagüey to Havana again for the same amount. I thought that was totally reasonable!

Or you could opt for a bicycle – everyone in Cuba owns one and that's mostly how they get around, especially in towns further out from Havana! I met a woman with a bike who told me that it takes two weeks to cycle around Cuba. If you are going to do this though, take your own spare parts along with you, for if you do break down or puncture a tyre the parts aren't readily available.

It is also now possible to hire motorbikes for touring, as well as local scooters.

AMERICANS, CUBA AND THE EMBARGO

For a US citizen, travelling to Cuba raises some difficulties – which thankfully I did not have to go through.

A US arms embargo was imposed on Cuba in 1958 during its revolutionary war, and this embargo was extended to US exports to Cuba in 1960, and then to imports from Cuba in 1962. The embargo in its later, more absolute forms, known as *el bloqueo* in Cuban Spanish, was imposed in retaliation to Castro nationalising American businesses and property of the Americans.

(Hang on a minute, here. Didn't Columbus 'discover' America in the form of a Caribbean island? If so, why aren't Cubans Americans? Well actually, they are. As speakers of Spanish and Portuguese sometimes point out *misère*, because I doubt very much that it will change anything, to use the word America as an English-language shorthand for the United States is inaccurate and even somewhat un-PC. Correct usage would insist that Cubans are Americans, as are Canadians and even the inhabitants of Tierra del Fuego. And to speak of going from 'America' to an island where Columbus made landfall involves an element of logical absurdity. Still, though many a word has been changed or tidied up because of political incorrectness, I think we English-speakers are pretty much stuck with this bad habit.)

It looked for a while as though the embargo would be lifted under President Obama: but now there's Trump. Who knows!

The embargo affects American travellers today. "Travel to Cuba for tourist purposes remains prohibited by statute" says the website of the US Embassy in Cuba, bluntly.

However, travel for non-tourism purposes is permitted under a special license from the US Department of the Treasury's Office of Foreign Assets Control (OFAC). There are twelve categories of authorised travel, into at least one of which a US citizen must show that their trip to Cuba falls, for such a licence to be granted.

As of the time of writing the list of reasons for which travel might be allowed seems broad and humane. It includes such obvious matters as family reunions but also much else besides, including journalism, business, charitable work, sporting contacts and research. So, it might not be too hard for an American with a burning interest in the history, people or wildlife of Cuba to show that their trip met the requirements. Even writing this book might tick several boxes on the OFAC list if I were an American, I suppose.

But the fact that it is illegal for an American citizen to simply be a *tourist* in Cuba must be a show-stopper for most prospective visitors from a country that likes to style itself as the land of the free.

You can't use any American credit or debit cards in Cuba, everything for an American is cash only. The Cuban government also charges a 10% fee for all US money exchanged into Cuban CUC pesos, the 1:1 exchange rate notwithstanding.

The trade embargo is not absolute. There are blanket or licenced exceptions for things like books, food and medicine, plus a limited amount of US commerce on the island (also limited at the Cuban end lest capitalism re-establish itself), in addition to the loopholes for non-tourism travellers. At present, 6.6% of imports into Cuba come from the USA. Cuba has learned to manage very well without the USA, or almost without the USA. But obviously, the island would do better if key elements of trade and tourism could be freed up.

In 2014, the United Nations General Assembly held a vote in which 188 countries out of 193 voted against the ongoing embargo, which many regard as punitive and vindictive given that the Cuban Missile Crisis was a long time ago now and given that the Cuban regime is very far from having been the worst dictatorship ever to have established itself in the Americas, many of the worst having been US-backed dictatorships in places like Chile, Guatemala, and for that matter, in Cuba itself.

Human rights charities like Amnesty International and Human Rights Watch have been very critical of the embargo and encourage any moves away from it. They have not been clamouring for the US to maintain the squeeze on Cuba in the hope that human rights will improve, feeling that the embargo hurts ordinary people more than it helps.

Indeed, it's hard to avoid the impression that the embargo might even have helped to prop up the regime and maintain its radicalism over a period of several decades in a sort of London-in-the-Blitz sense. For a Latin American leader, there is just about no local downside in being seen to stand up to the 'Americans' and to identify him- or herself with heroes of past struggles for independence from the Spaniards or the Portuguese. Even right-wing Latin American leaders have had to be careful not to be seen to be too obviously in Washington's pocket.

In a Cuba more recently independent than countries on the mainland which became independent in Napoleonic times, and where, as a result, revolution and national pride seem to be in the blood to an even greater extent than in those countries, the more the USA squeezed, the tougher the nut got. And that's another reason to end the embargo, I suspect.

GENERAL INFORMATION

CURRENCY

As I have noted, there are two main forms of currency in Cuba, one for locals and one for foreigners. The CUC or Cuban convertible pesos is equivalent to US Dollars (USD), so 1 CUC = 1 USD.

The second currency is for locals only, although a visitor can sometimes get hold of it. The Cuban national peso (CUP) is worth only a few cents US, so 1 CUC peso is worth roughly 26 CUP pesos. That way, the authorities can charge what is in effect two prices for some of the everyday essentials of life, a high price for foreigners and a low price for locals.

Hard to get your head around? Don't worry most prices are in the Cuban convertible pesos until you head outside of the main cities. Just be aware that the $ stands for both, as well as the USD, but that in this book I am using the $, as I mentioned earlier, to refer to the tourist / traveller currencies of CUC and USD. One $ is one USD if I am talking about an internet purchase; but one CUC, in cash, if I am talking about local transactions.

CLOTHES, CUSTOMS AND CLIMATE

I mentioned the frustrations of not having a hot shower available to warm up underneath. Yes, it does get cold around the time of year I visited, in December and January. Cuba is in the tropics, but only just. So, it has summer and winter seasons: and waves of extreme Canadian cold and ice storms that have blown southward, like the one that froze the O-rings on the space shuttle in 1986, causing it to blow up, will sometimes keep going across the tropical line and the Florida Strait that divides Florida from Cuba.

After all, they've made it all the way from Canada, already. Cuba's only just a little further on.

Also, Cuba has many mountain areas that a visitor might wish to see, and they get even colder than low-lying areas. Thus, and especially in the northern-hemisphere winter months, it pays to pack some warm clothing and sensible shoes. And sometimes, even Viazul buses can be a bit too aggressively air-conditioned.

Lastly, as befits an old Latin culture, Cubans can sometimes be quite formal. Everything is not all dancing and salsas. Shorts and sandals and a T-shirt won't get you in everywhere, no matter what the thermometer reads. So, bring some smart clothes, as well.

PUBLIC TOILETS AND WATER

If you go to use a public toilet you have to pay $1 and there is no toilet paper or soap! The further rural you go, the more you have to watch what you eat. Three of the women on the bus from Baracoa had chronic diarrhoea (including me).

You can buy treated drinking water, or do it yourself using the sun to sterilise the water – quite a handy trick I've learnt, convenient for the traveller but a lifesaving technique for people in poor tropical countries without access to good water or facilities for boiling bad water. This is called the SODIS method and involves leaving suspect water out in strong sunshine for six hours in a clear PET bottle, until a combination of heat and ultraviolet radiation kills any germs that might be present. It doesn't work with muddy water nor bottles made of other materials that block the ultraviolet radiation, and it's best to read up independently on how to do it properly, but that is the essence of it.

CUBAN COMMUNISM – HOW IT AROSE; WHY IT PERSISTS; WILL IT LAST?

Cuba is still a Communist country, unlike many others that have reverted to a more market economy, and many things are controlled by the government.

People in Cuba are very pro-communism, for them it works. While we might struggle to understand how doctors are only on $20 — that is to say, a bit over 500 national pesos — a month, they struggle to understand how they are so well paid in our countries. It's quite often the case in Communist countries past and present that housing is laid on for free or at least at an incredibly cheap rate. This is one of the hidden attractions of such a regime, a powerful incentive to stay in a Communist country and put up with meagre salaries and a certain lack of freedom, for after all, everybody has to have somewhere to live. Equally, by the same token, out-of-control housing costs are a Western Achilles Heel at present, along with unemployment.

That's the situation today. How did Cuba end up going Communist in the first place? Oddly enough, the revolutionary movement led by Fidel Castro that swept to power on the first of January 1959, wasn't a Communist movement at all. The Movement of the 26th of July, as it was called, after an earlier, failed attempt to overthrow the US-backed dictator Fulgencio Batista on the 26th of July 1953 only proposed middle-of-the-road and democratic reforms, and gained most of its popular support from the fact that Batista was becoming increasingly murderous, repressive and unpopular.

Even the Americans did not support Batista in the end, and Castro and some of his associates toured the USA in triumph in March and April 1959. Relations between the Castro regime and the USA were reasonably good to begin with, though strained by the fact that the Castro regime had hundreds of Batista's henchmen shot. Like Maximilien Robespi-erre in revolutionary Paris, the Castroites justified such executions by saying

34

HONORS LINCOLN—Cuban Prime Minister Fidel Castro poses at the Lincoln Memorial where he laid a wreath below statue of the Civil War President.
(AP Wirephoto)

CASTRO TELLS HIS ELECTIONS STAND

WASHINGTON, April 19 (AP) — Prime Minister Fidel Castro said tonight his provisional Cuban government "does not want to stay in power one minute longer than is necessary before having free elections."

Clarifying remarks made earlier on a nationwide television appearance, Castro made the comment after a two hour and 20 minute discussion with Vice-President Nixon at the Capitol.

The bearded Castro

He said he did not have an opportunity to explain on television one point about Cuban elections "as well as I should have liked."

Castro told his TV questioners it might be four years before Cuba holds free elections. He had said previously that elections would be held in two years.

He said his lengthy talk with Nixon — originally scheduled for 15 minutes — had been "very friendly."

"I tell you this as true,"

Fragment of a front page Los Angeles Times *lead for a story continued inside, 20 April 1959*

that things would have been even worse if they had simply handed the Batista-ites over to a vengeful mob whose catch-cry was *al paredón*, 'to the wall'. But at any rate, the Castro regime was not seen as being actually Communist to begin with.

Nevertheless, hard-liners in the Castro regime did not trust the honeymoon with the USA to last. They pointed to the tragic case of Guatemala, which had instituted middle-of-the-road reforms between 1944 and 1954, with the country's first-ever peaceful and democratic transition of power taking place in that decade, only to have its infant liberal-democracy overthrown by a small band of far-right rebels landed in Guatemala by the American CIA, after the CIA had first made sure that the Guatemalan armed forces would not fight back. The chief hard-liner in the Cuban revolution was Che Guevara, who had been in Guatemala when the elected government was overthrown by the Americans.

As in Cuba, and for that matter the Philippines when it passed into US control, the real issue in Guatemala was land reform and the way that large Spanish holdings descended from conquistador times – *latifundia*, a word that also has connotations of 'plantation' and 'monoculture' – had not been broken up and transferred to the peasantry but had instead merely passed to local elites and then to American agribusiness corporations, when then enlisted the support of the US government and military to resist the 'Communism' of land redistribution.

Ironically, major land redistribution *was* carried out under American auspices after World War II in the three main parts of the former Japanese Empire that fell under American control, namely Japan proper, South Korea and Taiwan, then known as Formosa. This was done in order to weaken the power of the large landowners, a military-aristocratic stratum who were seen as *the* problem in pre-war Japanese society. If the class of great lords and samurai were to lose its economic base, more modern and peaceful attitudes would come to prevail in the former Japanese empire, and so things have largely turned out.

By way of a colossal double standard, no such reforms of the system established by the conquistadores was undertaken in the former Spanish possessions that fell under US control. The commercial temptation to simply take over the plantations as a going concern seems to have been too great, and, of course, the Americans had judged themselves to be more benevolent rulers than the samurai or the conquistador. That the system was otherwise structurally the same, still one of great lords ruling over a particularly downtrodden sort of peasantry, even if the lords now wore business suits rather than suits of armour, escaped their notice.

In an important 1961 speech[1] Che Guevara contended, in tones almost identical to American attitudes toward the Japanese military aristocracy, that, with regard to the first liberating revolutions of the nineteenth century, the problem was that these early revolutions had not broken up the large conquistador estates created by Spanish monarchy.

The urban bourgeoise or middle class, potentially a progressive force, liberal and scientific in temper in more advanced countries, was weak in Latin American countries and allied itself with the large rural landowners and their reactionary politics, against the poor. Worse yet, the United States had installed itself as the even more powerful successor to the Spanish monarchy via agri-business firms that had bought up conquistador estates as going concerns, not hesitating even to overturn elected regimes that sought to return the land to the tiller. As such, there was no hope of social progress in such countries other than a thoroughgoing revolution, even if moderate and electoral reforms were possible elsewhere.

Interestingly enough, it *is* the case that Communist and revolutionary regimes have almost always come to power in backward countries where social progress seems to be blocked, and almost never in industrially advanced countries, as Karl Marx supposed they would. So, by implication, Cold War America was making a rod for its own back by supporting large landowning interests inherited from earlier conquistador-like eras in the nations of the Third World, landowning interests that were on the wrong side of history in these countries. Third World revolutionary movements in the 1960s fed on America's negative energy. It was all a bit like the plot of the 1950s sci-fi classic *Forbidden Planet*, with the Americans as the space explorers and Third World Communism as the Id-Monster that fed on the

1 'Cuba: Historical Exception or Vanguard in the Revolutionary Struggle?' (9 April 1961).

hostility of those who fought against it; even if Guevara did not put the matter quite like that!

Guevara had some proof to back up his large claims about the fundamental need to return conquistador land to the tillers and the way that the Americans were frustrating this otherwise natural and necessary development. In early-1950s Guatemala, President Jacobo Árbenz, elected in 1951, had tried to redistribute currently-unused fruit-company land to the peasantry. Vast areas of land stood idle in 1950s Guatemala with the commercially-minded owners only cultivating the most profitable bits, while much of the population was undernourished. Árbenz thought it would be a win-win solution if the less profitable land were given to the peasants to grow food for themselves upon, and maybe some things to sell in the market. The existing landowners were compensated with government bonds. But even this rather mild and almost obvious initiative seems to have been viewed as too radical by Árbenz's enemies – who probably regarded it as the thin edge of the red wedge – and Árbenz was duly overthrown. In Cuba, the landowning corporations expropriated by the Castros had often undervalued their operations to get out of paying local taxes. When the Cuban revolution came, the corporations found that this trick came back to bite them because compensation was offered at that book value. Perhaps the same was true in Guatemala as well.

The Guatemalan coup of 1954 had a massively radicalising effect on Guevara, who was in that country at the time and who resolved that future reformers and revolutionaries in Latin America would gain nothing by trying to meet the United States or local elites halfway.

(In strictly military terms the Guatemalan coup of 1954, which took the form of an un-resisted invasion by CIA-sponsored filibusters, was the template for the later Bay of Pigs invasion of Cuba in 1961: an invasion which failed because the Cuban armed forces *did* fight back. The original plan for the Bay of Pigs invasion, formulated under US President Eisenhower, had also called for a pre-planned formal intervention by the Organisation of American States, led by the USA, in the event that the invasion was not an instant success: a belt-and-braces approach. President Kennedy was not willing to countenance that part of the plan, and that was another reason why the 1961 Bay of Pigs invasion was doomed.)

As the Americans themselves would later admit, offering a formal apology under President Clinton in 1999, the Guatemalan coup of 1954 had been an unmitigated historical disaster not only for the people of Guatemala, for whom democracy had been replaced by decades of particularly appalling oppression, but also for the USA itself since it did so much to fuel suspicion of American intentions across the region and indeed across the world. A pre-existing tendency toward anti-Americanism in many countries, which was grounded in acts of cultural insensitivity, had been made more militant and political by the Guatemalan coup: and obviously not without reason.

But in 1959, any admission along those lines still lay in the future. And so, the hard-liners of the revolution argued that Cuba might as well be hung for a sheep as for a lamb. The USA was bound to attack sooner or later in order to try and put the usual bunch of crooks and great landowners back in charge. That being so, the Cuban revolution needed a protector. This protector could only be the Soviet Union.

To reiterate, behind the immediately suspicious attitudes, there was a longer history of anti-Americanism in Cuba stemming from ethnic and cultural insults, most of them unconscious and thoughtless in nature, that Cuba had suffered at the hands of the Americans from the snubbing of García on 17 July 1898 pretty much all the way down to the 1950s.

As it can be seen, nothing good ever comes of racism, nor from more 'colourblind' assumptions of cultural superiority ('American exceptionalism' / 'manifest destiny' / 'the indispensable nation'), which look much the same to outsiders. Such attitudes have a strong tendency to produce blowback and disaster in the end. Along with a tendency to make enemies of reformers, a tendency to insult other cultures has been the great weakness or blind spot of the United States, the source of endless resentment-fuelled 'blowback'.

And so, revolutionary Cuba spiralled into the Communist camp in ways that were ultimately 'Made in America', an ironic twist on the old 'House Brand' cartoon.

Even so, all that was sixty years ago, now. Also, the causes of all this past misunderstanding are reasonably well known these days. Fast forwarding to the present day, why is it that it has taken so long for relations between the USA and Cuba to be normalised?

Why has the regime endured such harsh sanctions from the USA for so long. And, why is it that it has survived as a Communist regime for so long at the same, when others not subject to sanctions fell?

It's hard to avoid the impression that at least some of the longstanding hostility is due to Cuba's radical chic, an ability to make revolution, rebellion and resistance look sexy in ways that have provoked the Americans and driven them up the wall.

Most of the world's population, quite possibly, has seen Cuban government photographer Alejandro Korda's famous picture of Che Guevara looking heroic – an image Korda named 'Guerillero Heroico' – if only on T-shirt. But as we can see from the next pair of photographs, Guevara certainly wasn't the only charismatic revolutionary in 1950s Cuba.

If the revolution and its causes were ultimately made in America, by the same token, it's hard to avoid the impression that the whole 1960s look, and

Vilma Espin (with 26th July armband), and Camilo Cienfuegos.

These photographs are very widely reproduced on the web in low-resolution formats
without attribution; originals are probably Cuban official copyright, all rights reserved.

attitude, was made in Cuba and exported to the rest of the world, including
American inner cities and college campuses. And it's just as hard to avoid the
impression that this got under official America's skin to an almost unique
degree as the 1950s became the 1960s and beyond.

Stodgy Eastern European Communists, totally foreign Chinese ones or
risible North Korean ones were never going to make very many converts
among the young people of the Western Hemisphere: but there was
something far more subversive about the Cuban sort. One American official
quoted in a British *Guardian* newspaper story about Fidel Castro and his
many narrow escapes from bungling assassins egged on by the White House
said that "Cuba seems to have the same effect on American administrations
that a full moon has on a werewolf. We may not sprout hair and howl but
we behave in the same way."[2]

2   Quoted in Duncan Campbell, 'Close but No Cigar: how America failed to kill Fidel
Castro', *The Guardian*, 26 November 2016.

41

The same defiant, piratical qualities that made the Cuban revolutionaries subversive abroad, also solidified their support at home. Thus, the Cubans live under Communism but imagine themselves to be freer than other people because their regime was indeed founded by romantic-looking bandits, in effect.

There are many who argue that Cuban radical chic is actually responsible for the demise of the left. People like Joe Klein in Newsweek have argued that it helped style to triumph over substance on the left after 1965 or thereabouts. Old-style leftist goals such as full employment, affordable housing and the right to join a trade union were forgotten about while feckless baby-boomer hipsters grew their hair long and put on a Che Guevara T-shirt. There's some merit to that claim too, of course.

The association of long hair and freedom notwithstanding, the Communists apply strict laws to the people of Cuba: though that you may or may not notice while travelling there. The government allows people to run their own businesses on the basis they are small – very small – and even then, they have to pay extraordinarily high taxes. Taxes are something the people of Cuba do not like – they have never had to pay them prior to the boom in the tourist industry; more about this later on.

Until recently, Cuban people were not allowed to stay in hotels and accommodation set aside for tourists – they had to stay in the communist or government run establishments.

Everything is censored: the internet, TV shows, movies, books, magazines and newspapers by the government. To put the access to internet into perspective, only 1.6% of the population has it. Not every place in Cuba has internet readily available: you need to be wary of that when travelling around, even as a tourist.

Something else that really amazed me is that Cubans cannot change jobs or careers without government permission. While it may be shocking for me, and maybe you too, it's just how they live and they seem happy and content with it.

Cuba is not a Western Society. Some people can't hack it and go to Cuba to be totally shocked and then leave. I think that's part of being a 'Maverick' traveller – you stop and think. I loved talking to all the people I met: the locals and other tourists give you interesting perspectives. It's well worth remembering we don't all think the same, after all.

I would definitely recommend tipping the staff – the cleaners, the cooks all the people behind the scenes. They are the one who don't make much out of the tourist ventures.

Finally, it must be said that Cuba is going through a transitional period, with Raúl Castro the current President stepping down in 2018. Raúl is the last of the Castros, and this will surely open a whole can of worms regarding the question of who will step into fill his shoes and whether they will be as faithful to the Castro legacy, or not.

CHAPTER THREE

High Heels and Hiking in Havana

H ELLO Havana! I was seriously in for an eye opening. You can take everything you think you know about Havana or Cuba in general and throw it out the window.

Everyone who goes to Havana (Habana in Spanish) has to go to the Malecón – the amazing seaside walk in sight of the conquistador-era fortress of El Morro, where the ocean pounds against an ever crumbling and eroding stone wall. It should be if it isn't already a Havana tradition to get drenched by sea spray as you casually stroll along, I knew I would be visiting the Malecón a few times!

I've been mentioning how it can get cold in Cuba, from north winds especially. In fact, the first 500 metres of the Malecón was built by American

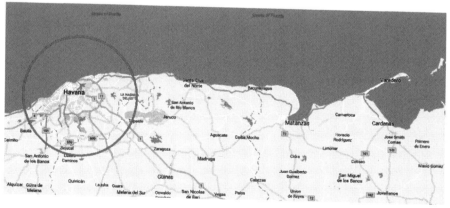

Havana, on the north coast of Cuba. Map Data ©2017 Google, INEGI

A must-do in Havana. Stroll along the Malecón and get battered by rogue waves while looking out to the amazing El Morro fortress.

The name means 'the Promontory' and refers to a rocky headland on which the fortress itself, more formally known as *El Castillo de los Tres Reyes Magos del Morro*, sits. The full name means the Castle of the Three Wise Kings (as in the Bible), of 'the Promontory'. The tower is a lighthouse added in 1846, the *Faro Castillo del Morro*.

engineers in the first years of the 20th century, when Cuba was briefly a sort of protectorate of the USA — the US base at Guantánamo dates back to that era — in order to safeguard central Havana from wild seas stirred up by the storms known locally as *nortes*, or 'northers'.

Later Cuban governments extended the promenade to a length of 8 km. Even so, it's surprising that such a prominent Havana landmark as the Malecón was begun by the Americans: who were no doubt anxious to demonstrate the difference between an energetic Teddy Roosevelt-era USA and centuries of supposed Spanish indolence. Along with the forts the Spaniards built, such artifacts put me in mind of the old Monty Python line, 'What have the Romans ever done for us?'

The Malecón is officially known today as the Avenida de Maceo in honour of Lt. General José Antonio de la Caridad Maceo y Grajales, the 'Bronze Titan', who was a black man and thus an exemplar of a still wider liberation struggle than the liberation of Cuba itself.

In his 1945 work *A Naturalist in Cuba*, the American biologist Thomas Barbour wrote that:

Two phenomena are so characteristic and dramatic that I cannot pass them by without a word. I recall the first of many northers which I have felt and seen in Havana. A norther is usually preceded by a south wind. Perhaps you know the saying: a Sur duro, Norte seguro. The south wind gradually dies out and there is a breathless stillness which somehow always seems to be to convey, subconsciously, an aura of impending trouble. Suddenly the norther, really a northwester, begins to blow; the temperature drops and there may be a drizzle or a sharp shower of rain. If you are in Havana my advice is to hurry to the Malacón [sic] and watch the ocean grow angry. If the norther is a really bad one you'll soon have to take shelter. Many a time I have seen the waves rise to dash and break, the spray flying over the lighthouse on Morro Castle. I have often seen the streets of the waterfront inundated in a few hours after the onset of the storm and when the tempest has died away seen gangs of workmen clearing away rifts of sand and coral heads tossed up by the waves into the sreets. The weather now may clear and a few days of fresh, cool weather ensue, most enjoyable wherever you may be. Sometimes, however, the succeeding days of cold may bring great suffering to people who live in houses where there is no glass in the windows and no blankets on the beds. The northers are the exciting feature of winter weather and they form a contrast to the hurricanes of the summer months.[1]

1   From a longer quote in Patricia Dunlavy Valenti, *Understanding the Old Man and the Sea: A Student Casebook . . .* Westport CT, Greenwood Press, 2002, pp. 32-33. The mis-spelling of Malecón as Malacón was observed in the source just described and may not be present in the original.

The Malecón in winter

All this was yet before me when I found myself at the boarding gate at Miami International Airport on the afternoon of the 28th of December, three days before New Year's Eve. I would be arriving at 4:30 p.m. at José Martí International Airport in Havana. I had my backpack arranged with lighter clothing and although Miami was warm, I was looking forward to the Cuban heat and the 80% humidity that was expected. I had my guide books ready and was fervently flicking through them on the plane, making sure I hadn't missed anything.

José Martí International Airport, outside Havana.
Piviso image, CC0 public domain

The José Martí International Airport was a pleasant surprise, it was somewhat more modern than I had presumed. It had flat-screen information displays just like a modern airport, not the older boxy-TV ones.

There are three terminals in the airport mostly accommodating air traffic from the USA and domestic flights, with a fourth terminal planned. The terminals are really spread out so you definitely want to make sure of what one you are flying out of or into before getting there. I was surprised by the

'Havana: The City of Columns'. Shady colonnades are a feature of Havana's older architecture. The Swiss-born Cuban author Alejo Carpentier gave the city its familiar nickname.

number of charter flights booked to and from the airport. The international airport is in the suburb of Rancho Boyeros, about 25 kilometres south west of downtown Havana, so it isn't too far into town.

There was an hour-long queue to change money. I spotted a credit card machine that worked for me, but it would not work for an American as American bank accounts are blocked from their end, as part of the US trade embargo. If you can get CUC pesos outside Cuba, or have a non-US bank account, that is a big help in getting through the airport quickly.

I grabbed my bag, made it through customs with no issues and went in search of transport to get me into town to find some accommodation.

The second the doors opened to let travellers out of the air-conditioned airport, heat and humidity hit me like a wave Anyway, I eventually got a taxi and that's when I saw my first reference to Cuba being 'old fashioned': the car I got would have been from the early 1950's. It was a fabulous trip into the city, my head was just constantly swivelling around and the taxi driver was kind enough to give me a mini- commentary in his broken English. First lesson learnt though – airport taxi rides are expensive! I think the trip equated to about $30 and it was only 30 minutes from the airport in to the city of Havana. We travelled along a motorway, which again confounded my expectations. I didn't expect a motorway even if Havana was the capital city. Once the motorway ended we had to proceed through a maze of narrow streets big enough for one car to pass through. That was rather more in line with what I had been expecting. It seemed as though Havana and perhaps by implication the whole of Cuba itself was modern in patches – modern here and there – with a sort of older world in between.

Indeed, where other countries lack historical buildings and fascinating architecture, Cuba has it all still, perfectly preserved in time. You will not find sky-scrapers and tall concrete apartments that block out the sun here (or, not very many of them anyway): just attention-grabbing architecture from a bygone era. I fell in love with the city immediately: Havana was like the shiniest jewel in a Cuban crown full of them. Everything was vibrant; the city was alive with smells and colour – loads of it. The colonial-style buildings were not our standard Auckland grey but pastel shades of pink and blue. My immediate thought was: Havana = Fun.

Havana is such a walkable city! Not only do the streets follow an easy grid with few blind alleys, but there are many orientation guides in the streets of the tourist areas, so it is easy to find your way around.

51

Havana really surprised! I spent a lot of time in the district of Havana an area called La Habana Vieja or Old Havana, a UNESCO World Heritage site. Next time I visit I will definitely spread my wings a bit and check out the other areas more.

The central urban area of Havana is divided into three municipalities, each with an English and Spanish version of the name, Central Havana (Centro Habana), Vedado, and Old Havana (La Habana Vieja). Old Havana is at the eastern end of the Malecón, Vedado at the western end, and Central Havana behind the central area of the Malecón.

Central Havana is where the city takes on a modern twist; it's where tourist agencies and businesses operate out of. Then there's the 'party' area as I'd call it in Vedado – it used to be a bit of a dodgy area but it's all been cleaned up a bit now and is bursting with some top-notch restaurants and a lively restaurant and pub scene.

Old Havana sits right in the heart of the city – a proud display of everything that makes Cuba so unique. It's a place to appreciate the old buildings, statues and solid looking fortresses that appear around every corner – like I said Havana is full of surprises!

The layout of Old Havana (and indeed most of main urban area) was great for getting around on foot, with long, straight, handsome avenues, straight streets branching off them, and small square blocks only 100m or so on a side.

I went to all four of the main squares in Old Havana: the Plaza de Armas, Plaza Vieja, Plaza de San Francisco de Asís and Plaza de la Catedral.

Within Old Havana there are over 900 buildings that hold significant historical importance, and are really unique for their baroque and art deco styles.

Hotel Saratoga, Plaza Vieja, interior of chapel, street scene near Capitol

Havana Street Scenes

Capitolio Nacional and Gran Teatro de la Habana, on Paseo Martí.

Top photograph by Michael Oswald, Wikimedia Commons, CC0 public domain, taken 29 December 2004. Bottom photograph is a public domain image by 'Canadaolympic989', Wikimedia Commons, March 2006 (Architecturally rectified and cropped slightly for this book).

THE PEOPLE WHO LIVED IN CUBA BEFORE HAVANA WAS FOUNDED

The main indigenous inhabitants of the Bahamas, Cuba, Hispaniola, Jamaica and Puerto Rico were people called Taíno. As with many indigenous groups in the Americas the Taíno, who also dwelt in parts of Florida and coastal South America. Politically, the Taino lived under rulers called caciques, each of whom ruled an area called a cacicazgo, itself divided into twenty or so local units at the village level called nitaínos. The word 'Taíno' means a virtuous person; thus, the Taino considered themselves to be the virtuous people.

Technologically, the Taíno made fine pottery and knew how to farm the land. On Cuba, there were twenty-nine recently-established caciazgos at the time of Columbus, and five caciazgos of longer standing on Hispaniola, the true stronghold of Taíno culture in its most organised form, where perhaps one million Taíno lived. In Taíno the word Cuba means the place where land is abundant: a sort of frontier in other words, a place where Taíno culture existed in a simpler form and was becoming more organised when the Spanish arrived.

Words we associate with the Caribbean such as barbecue, canoe, hammock and hurricane also come from the Taíno language.

Rather unfairly, in view of the numbers and wide reach of the Taíno in 1492, the Caribbean would get its name from a less numerous people who lived mainly on its lesser islands, the Carib. This curious amnesia may reflect the fact that the Taíno were assimilated into the wider population on the larger islands of the Caribbean with astonishing rapidity. It was long thought that the Taíno were almost wiped out physically, in the main by smallpox. However, a recent survey showed that 61 per cent of the population of

Puerto Rico had Taíno blood (or Taíno mitochondrial DNA to be more precise), so the extermination was more cultural than physical on Puerto Rico, at least.

There is only one place in Cuba where identifiably surviving Taíno communities still exist, at Baracoa in the east. In contrast, the Carib survived into modern times in better shape, perhaps because the many small islands they inhabited underwent less transformation by colonists and were less susceptible to European plagues. After 1550, any recognisably indigenous people that European sailors ran into in the Caribbean were likely to be Carib, not Taíno.

There is another indigenous group that is said to have existed in Cuba. On the basis of limited contact made by Columbus and things the Taíno had said, the conquistador Diego Velázquez de Cuéllar reported that in the far west of Cuba there were people who lived in an Edenic state of nature, "in the manner of savages, for they have neither houses nor village quarters, nor field, nor do they eat anything else but the flesh they take in the mountains and turtles and fish." The inhabitants of these regions were said to live in caves, to be literal cave-men or cave-people. I will henceforth refer to this conquistador as Diego Velázquez for short and for simplification in line with English naming customs and less formal Spanish usage as well, in which people usually only have one surname and not two.

Such were the people called Guanahacabibe (also known as Guanahatabey), the same word that is used to describe Guanahacabibe Peninsula and Guanahacabibe Peninsula National Park at the western tip of the main island of Cuba. Archaeologists confirm that the Guanahacabibe were 'aceramic' meaning that they did not make or use pottery. On the other hand, this does not necessarily mean life in a complete state of nature. New Zealand Māori were aceramic at the time of Captain Cook as well, but the way of life of most Māori in 1769 was otherwise quite similar to that of most of the Taíno in 1492. Not much else is really known about the Guanahacabibe and it is quite possible that they were simply Taíno beachcombers, leading a simpler life than other Taíno.

HAVANA'S HISTORY

Havana was founded in 1514 by the aforementioned Diego Velázquez, who is regarded as the original founder of a number of Cuba's cities. The name San Cristóbal de la Habana was bestowed upon Velázquez's settlement by another Spanish conquistador named Pánfilo de Narváez. The city centre, which must have been little more than a camp in the early days,

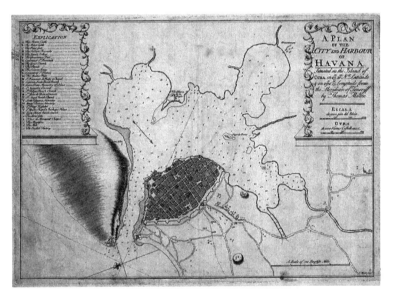

Eighteenth-century 'Plan of the City and Harbour of Havana'.

The harbour entrance and future Malecón are at bottom left in this plan, though they lie to the north. The city shown corresponds very much to the Old City of modern Havana. (British Library)

was relocated at least twice and eventually fixed in place next to Havana's natural harbour in 1519. The name San Cristóbal means St. Christopher, while the meaning of la Habana (Havana) is obscure, but thought to be of Taíno origin and to perhaps refer to an indigenous chief of that time and place, Habaguanex. Alternatively, it might be a borrowing from Dutch, meaning haven or harbour.

The city became one of Spain's most strategic strongholds near the Gulf of Mexico, with a sheltered natural harbour on the mouth of the Río Mayabeque.

Havana did not become the capital city of Cuba until 1607, replacing the previous capital of Santiago de Cuba, which is located on the south coast. Havana was frequently attacked by pirates, which led to some interesting history and even more interesting influences in architecture. That led to the construction of some of the oldest forts in the Caribbean, the La Punta and El Morro forts were built in the late 1500s and early 1600s, and you can still see them proud and intact there today, from the Malecón.

The Seven Years War tested the Spanish defences when in 1762 British ships attacked Havana, first laying siege to El Morro. The Spanish forces were defeated and this brought in another influence – the British had control of Cuba for just under a year. The Spanish sought reconciliation and exchanged the future US state of Florida for Cuba, after which Spain increased the lines of defence in Havana. Havana was to become one of the most fortified cities in the New World.

Havana became a trading port, shipping sugar, rum, coffee and tobacco to other cities developed by Spain and even further afield. At the beginning of the 1900s Havana was increasing in technology and began expanding as its 250,000 population grew rapidly.

*Comandancia General of the Policia Nacional
Revolutionaria, located in an old Spanish castle.
And yes, that is a drawbridge across a moat,
although these days the bridge is permanent.*

Its close proximity to the United States saw many wealthy Americans set up camp in and around the city. Casinos opened, and the introduction of gambling laid out a more serious and darker side. When Fidel Castro came to power, his goal was to share out the wealth equally among the people. He sent the Americans packing and gave the once-glamorous hotels to the poor to inhabit.

With the ever-changing economy in Cuba and the reality that the US enforced embargo may not last forever, Havana and Cuba are coming alive. Like Cinderella, from rags to riches!

* * *

My first stop in Havana was a casa particular, run by a guy named Carlos whom a fellow traveller recommended for his hostel and guide services. Carlos ran Mango Hostel where he rented out a bed for $8 a night. Carlos was interesting. He was running this hostel in Havana but his cousin had left to go to America to make money. At the time his cousin moved, it was a bit easier for Cuban people to go between the two countries than it is now. Cuban emigres to the USA used to be welcomed, but now they need visas. Carlos said his cousin's family was having trouble settling in. Facing long hours and poorly paid work, they were considering moving back to Havana.

Carlos told me he could understand why his cousin's family left and why some people are still leaving, and yet also why they were thinking of coming back. There is widespread poverty in Cuba: but it is of an equally-shared kind, and not especially insecure or socially stigmatising in the way that being poor is in the USA. Basic needs are met by the government in Cuba, and most people are in the same boat.

Most people, that is: if you have a job in the tourism industry, you can do very well for yourself. In fact, the Cuban government announced in 2013 that it was going to do away with the dual currency system whereby someone working in tourism and earning CUC pesos could be better off than a doctor paid in CUP pesos. On the other hand, they have not done so yet, perhaps because it is tourism itself that is the issue, not the dual currency system. Tourists would simply exchange their foreign money for fantastic amounts of CUP pesos if there were no CUC pesos, leading to inflation and even worse social tensions.

There is no easy solution to the distortions caused by tourism apart from the development of the rest of the Cuban economy. This should not be too difficult given the high levels of education and health of the population and the generally honest administration of the island. But the easing of American sanctions is a precondition for any Cuban economic take-off, I imagine.

The whole reason why casas came about is that when post-revolutionary Cuba eventually opened up to tourists, they did not have enough accommodation anymore. The government asked the people to help out by opening up their own businesses in the form of casas particulares. So, that's what a lot of people did do. Whether it be a basic mattress on the floor and no hot showers or something more swept-up, they did it. Like much in Cuba the system of casas particulares might take a bit of getting used to but seems to work, after a fashion.

Anyway, when I arrived at the Mango Hostel I met Carlos at the entrance, and he simply told me "Oh, I have given your bed away just now, but I have a friend down the road".

So, I ended up walking down the road, and that's when I met Mikalena. That was to become a bit of a tradition for the rest of my time while staying in Cuba. You book a bed at a casa and then it's full, and they find you somewhere else. This happened to me five or six times, but that was okay: I put it all down to a real authentic experience of a different culture.

Other foreigners who expected their booking to be hard and fast found this sort of thing shocking and couldn't handle it; but to my mind Cuba is an experience of a different way of life, a way of life that seems to revolve around constant last-minute improvisation. You just have to handle the unexpected, learn to manage and adjust. It's not your typical western society, you are leaving western society. So, I decided to go with the flow, and that was the way it was going to be.

I learned that Mikalena managed the place alongside her ninety-year-old mother. Her sister had bought the beautiful Spanish style home in the old district of Havana and turned it into a casa.

Mikalena spoke a little English, and I spoke a little Spanish, which was great. We ended up communicating through sign language as well and her family spoke some more English, so that helped.

A lot of people didn't speak a lot of English. I knew that in Cuba the main language spoken there was Spanish, but it was different. Definitely not like the Spanish dialects spoken in Spain.

It was amazing staying with Mikalena and her family, who were from Santiago de Cuba and full of information that only locals have! So, I learnt a thing or two. We got on really well, and Mikalena told me all about her mother who shared a downstairs room with her in the little casa. Her friend who helped her run the casa had a room upstairs, and they were both taking in international tourists. It cost anywhere between $20 to $45 per night and with four rooms to rent out they could make anywhere up to $140 a night: earnings which would go a long way in Cuba.

Everything is booked out in January and February, and their tourism has had a huge boost thanks to the introduction of Airbnb. Airbnb has also increased the prices for accommodation though. Mikalena said that the easing of travel restrictions on US visitors in March 2016 (though straight-out tourism remains technically illegal for US citizens), has also contributed to rising prices.

Staying in a casa is a true down-to-earth Cuban experience. Wooden chairs are a usual indicator of a casa home. I spent many evenings sitting in the chairs talking with Mikalena and her friends, sharing the occasional bottle of rum and listening to the collaboration of music from the bars and restaurants down the street. It really revealed to me the true nature of Cuban people and I think it gives you a real inside view into life living in Cuba. On top of that it was really relaxing and I was well looked after!

One topic Mikalena and I got talking about one time was the foo. I am always wary of what I eat overseas: the last thing I wanted was food poisoning! The US embargo on Cuban has had some noticeable effects on the people. Food was one I noticed straight away. The types of meals available varied on the availability of ingredients, when a restaurant or eatery ran out of something you just couldn't have it. When it would become available next was always a bit of a mystery.

I was surprised to discover that the food eaten by people in Havana is not spicy. The food was simple, and that was okay with me. Most produce is grown somewhere in the country and, more often than not, is organic – something we westerners have gone crazy for. I didn't feel like I had to look in any book to decide what food I wanted to eat, I found the food that I was eating amazing. I could get cooked sweet corn for $1. Sandwiches were aplenty, and salads too. The food in Havana was certainly enjoyable. But basically, if you stay at a casa particular you can also eat there for about $8 a night, and I have heard of people who have had some amazing food at their casa particular, especially seafood. The Cubans know how to cook seafood.

The nearer you get to Santiago de Cuba at the other end of the country; the more the food becomes spicy and hot. In general, though, the food in Havana was of a very good standard for anyone who does not like hot dishes.

Mikalena, the manager of the casa particular I stayed at in Havana

I had dinner at my casa particular the first night. It was lovely that they invited me: they didn't even charge me for dinner, but I provided some of my own food and bits and pieces. I ate pork with rice and beans, which is apparently a really popular meal in Cuba all round. There was also a lot of corn, which was great for me, being gluten-intolerant.

I was really surprised when Mikalena told me she only earned $15 a month (or a bit less than 400 national pesos a month) and her sister-in-law only earned $3. I was shocked, I thought

Social outing with Mikalena and her mother, Mikalena in my sunglasses
with some other Kiwis outside the Revolutionary Museum

$15 a month was pathetic and that she deserved more. So, I guess all the rest of the money they earned went to her sister. On top of her $15 a month earnings she would make extra cash by offering to do washing for guests and little things like that.

The average wage in Cuba is only $20 - $25 a month, or a bit more than what Mikalena was getting; and the more people I met from overseas the more I understood why they were visiting Cuba. With the emerging tourist industry, things were changing and everyone wanted to go there before it changed. There was an emerging middle class and these things, I think, are just beginning to become more noticeable.

Mikalena also told me her son was a doctor. He earned $20 a month but was looking at switching to the tourist industry because it was better paid. I met a lot of doctors while I was in Cuba, there is something like one doctor per 150 head of population.

Mikalena's casa didn't have Wifi and so I went in search of finding some one day and ran into a Nigerian doctor who was staying there. He was a character of sorts, in his mid-forties and rolling around with a beautiful Cuban woman who was a prostitute. He told me he was living

Havana has plenty of interesting architecture. At left, the Spanish Embassy in the Palacio Velasco; at right, a run-down but nonetheless solid-looking street frontage

in Queensland, had a wife there and also one in Canada! Anyway, the line at the local phone store called ETECSA (Empresa de Telecomunicaciones de Cuba S.A.), where you buy your Wifi cards, had at least fifty people waiting for the same thing. So, he said to his Cuban lady to go and buy me some, and she came back with twenty of these Wifi cards, so I was sorted for a wee while at least. He also talked to me about the rental car situation. He was leaving the next day back to Canada and had booked his rental car for when he came back in three months. He said it was easier to do it that way, booking while you were actually in the country rather than trying to do it online.

* * *

My first night in Havana had been good and I was looking forward to seeing more the following day. It was early in the morning after breakfast that I went out for a walk. The first thing I noticed was the people everywhere! All Cubans, with a few other tourists and travellers dotted here and there. It was an interesting contrast. Children playing games in the narrow streets bordered by these incredible buildings on either side. Laundry hung out to dry over balcony railings: it all added to an amazing impression of vitality.

I was just fascinated by the cars though – they were awesome and really throw you back a few decades! Back in 1955, Cuba was the biggest importer of American cars – hello embargo, and that stopped. Since then there have been no other imports from America so the cars are all classics, and well looked after by their owners as well. It'd be a classical car enthusiast's dream. People had to get creative: with no access to parts if anything went wrong the Cubans became inventive mechanics, and would add other car parts to keep them running. I thought it was brilliant! Apparently, at one point,

Castro banned people from on-selling their American-made cars – it seemed like a way to 'shame' them in my view.

I was amazed at the society Cuba had evolved into. There were no beggars or no homeless people. Yes, the wages were low, but it seemed that everyone had somewhere to live. I was surprised by the vibrancy of Havana; the sounds of some funky music somewhere in the distance became the background of our dinner, sometimes swallowed by the raucous laughter accompanied by our dinner conversations which ranged from food, to Fidel Castro, to single mothers and homelessness.

I would spend the next five days wandering around and exploring Havana, mostly in the older district. That was fine with me: there was plenty of interest to occupy my time.

I found myself at a book fair and I was amazed at all the old books they sold. I saw a few books by Miguel de Cervantes, the author of *Don Quixote* in the early 1600s, and other books and authors from the 18th and 19th Century. There were even old records, going way back! It was a great bit of nostalgia for me.

Cuba has been a huge hit with a lot of famous people over the years. In the 1930s and 1940s the writer Ernest Hemingway lived in a house called Finca la Vigía ('Lookout House'), which is now a museum dedicated to his memory with his famous fishing boat Pilar still parked outside, in the small town of San Francisco de Paula a short distance inland from Havana on a highway called the Carretera Central de Cuba. One of the downtown bars and restaurants made famous through long frequenting by Hemingway was El Floridita, where he sipped daiquiris and dreamed up his brilliant masterpieces. There is even a walking trail around the area of all the places connected to Hemingway and you can get a bus to Finca la Vigía: it's quite

El Floridita, where Ernest Hemingway hung out back in the day.

A bronze statue of Hemingway is placed at the bar inside. The building opposite is the Asturian Centre, which contains the international exhibitions of the National Museum of Fine Arts of Havana. Photograph by 'Miss Bono', Wikimedia Commons, CC-BY-3.0

a popular tourist attraction. Hemingway is really respected in Cuba and a prominent local figure there, up with Che and Castro.

Frank Sinatra was another one. He was introduced to Cuba by people in the Mafia when gambling and casinos were a part of the everyday scene in Havana. Most notoriously, Sinatra provided the entertainment at the 'Havana Conference' of leading American Mafia bosses, held at the Hotel Nacional de Cuba in December 1946. Ostensibly they'd all gone to Havana to watch Sinatra perform and it was just a coincidence they all went, that was their story and they stuck to it.

There are a number of Conquistador-era fortresses around Havana that make for a nice scenic stroll dipped in history.

The locals seemed to love Che Guevara – there were more pictures of him around then Fidel. The images were silhouettes and portraits of the leaders and I found them interesting rather them oppressive. A romantic figure, though regarded as ruthless by his enemies, Che was killed in Bolivia in 1967 fighting a rather hopeless guerrilla war. A couple of years before, he wrote to his parents that "Once again I feel under my heels the ribs of Rocinante," Don Quixote's horse. An inveterate revolutionary, Che was on the winning side in Cuba, but he couldn't win them all. And he knew it.

While he was alive, Fidel Castro seems to have preferred that such dead heroes be venerated instead of himself. When Fidel Castro died, there was not a single street in Cuba that bore his name, nor a single statue of him in Cuba.

Of course, Che is not the only revolutionary hero to be a sort of rock star to the Cubans by any means, as I mentioned earlier; though he is the best-known outside Cuba, largely as a result of the mass duplication of the iconic Alfredo Korda portrait, which began around the time of Che's death in 1967 and has never ceased. Korda allowed his slightly modified photograph of Che, which he called 'Guerillero Heroico', to be reproduced free of charge: and that was a large part of the secret of its success. The Che Guevara photo was the original viral product, before there was an Internet. But our T-shirts could just as easily have been graced by Cienfuegos, who was just as dreamy-looking as Che Guevara; or Vilma Espin, with her cheerful but martial look, reminiscent of a Soviet female sniper from World War II ('Viva Vilma', as one fan puts it).

Apart from modern icons of the revolution, I also noticed many statues dating back centuries around Havana. Founded in 1514, Havana really has a lot of history, as much as any European city has.

A ten-dollar taxi ride out to Tropicoco, and I found myself on some amazing surfing beaches. I found evidence of a folk-religion know as Santeria around the beaches. The locals had set up small shrines with dolls and shells. Apparently, people from Haiti had been brought to Cuba by the Spanish as slaves. The Haitian slaves, originally from Africa, brought with them the rites that would come to be known as Voodoo from Africa, and these became Santeria in the Spanish-speaking Caribbean. Haitians today prefer the French spelling Vodou, as it avoids the racist, lurid and over-dramatised connotations of the word Voodoo in English.

Cuban culture features a heavy influence of music: think salsa, rumba and trova genres. Walking around Old Havana I saw it firsthand. Street musicians beating out tunes on their drums, groups of singers harmonising on the street corners or all out dancers dressed head to toe in vibrant traditional dress shimmying around to the pleasure of the crowds. It is a place where you can seriously sit back and appreciate music and the talented people who drive it.

I did several strolls along the waterfront, where you could walk right alongside the ocean and got completely drenched as the waves crashed into the barriers. It was bliss, and the distant music that emanated from every shop added to the atmosphere.

The Malecón sits on the Northern coastal strip of Havana Central, and is a fast up and coming stretch of waterfront. It is an 8km stretch of concrete pathways along the coastline. While it is a bit of the rougher side, it is fast becoming the place to be. It's the kind of place you wander along with the wind in your hair, the salty spray on your face listening to music on your phone or just enjoying the buzz and noise that is Havana.

There were a lot of run-down buildings and homes adjoining the Malecón, but they were in the process of tidying this area up. Someone mentioned they were building more hotels there and restoring the old buildings in keeping with the character of Havana. One major benefit of

Havana: the Castillo de San Salvador de la Punta, across the harbour mouth from the larger El Morro castle.

recent tourism was that they had the money to do up these old buildings, which are the real treasures of Havana. I went for a quick tour through the nearby traditional port of Havana as well.

The booming tourism industry has meant the Cuban government has the funds to restore and keep all these beautiful national treasures well-kept. Many of Cuba's buildings and city centres are now listed on the UNESCO world heritage list, making it a goldmine for historical architecture.

It was around this area you got close up to the old forts built by the Spanish, the El Morro and a few others that sit like ancient watchful eyes over the harbour and the city.

One thing you can do in Havana, which I ran out of time to do, is to catch a ferry that takes you on tours around the harbour and islands.

In Havana, you don't really need to take a bus around, it's very easy to walk around - it's a very walkable city. You can take a bus out to the beach, which is a half an hour ride. It's hard to find bikes to hire, and I didn't see many motorbikes either.

One thing with walking in Havana is that it is completely safe to walk around on your own. A single woman myself, I am always wary of walking alone at night, but it was fine. The Cuban men liked to whistle at me while I walked past but I paid them no attention, or, if I caught their eye I'd just give a polite nod or wave and continue on. No one followed me and no one harassed me – that was fine.

The people of Cuba are genuine and friendly. Half or more seem to come from mixed ethnic backgrounds, from colonial influences and the infamous slavery industry. It is a vibrant bubbly mix of some of the most beautiful people I have ever met, and I felt safe at all times.

Closer views of Havana's Morro Castle, with Faro (lighthouse).

Top photograph Piviso image, CC0 public domain. *Bottom photograph* by Dr Anthony R. Picciolo, NOAA NODC, Wikimedia Commons, CC0 Public Domain, taken 1957

Havana Cathedral

A historical tableau painted on a wall

Fruit is popular in Havana and in Cuba in general, and cries 'tropical'! There were bananas (usually fried), mangoes, papaya and pineapples all available at little stalls on the side of the road. I caught their strong aromas wafting in the air as I strolled down the streets.

So, there I was wandering among the streets and stalls, buying sweetcorn that was beautiful and juicy from roadside carts and having an overall brilliant time. I felt like I danced everywhere, there was certainly a spring in my step that I hadn't expected.

I found Cuba was still getting itself organised in terms of coming to terms with an influx of foreigners. As I have mentioned, they have the two different currencies for the locals and for the travellers. For many goods and services the same price is charged in the two currencies, so that a foreigner would pay 6 CUC pesos for entry to the Revolutionary Museum in Havana and a local 6 CUP pesos. Thus, the dual currency system and ridiculously low local salaries are opposite faces of the same coin, no pun intended. Cuba is limited in terms of its economy by the embargo, so they make their money by visitors. Locals live cheaper and we pay to be a guest in their country – fair enough because the costs were not dramatic as far as I was concerned, even in CUC pesos.

Another day, I went looking for somewhere that had internet and found myself wandering aimlessly for a few hours. I had to do some work while I was on holiday, mostly in the form of checking my emails, so finding good reliable Wifi became an adventure in itself. It is as scarce as hen's teeth and finding Wifi outside of Havana I soon learned was even more difficult than I had thought. You are limited to a certain amount of data usage and you only get allocated 30 minutes at a time. Some of the hotels had Wifi and others didn't.

I couldn't access Google Drive because the data requirements were too big, which was frustrating at first. All I wanted to do was write a blog entry. Wifi is not everywhere yet, though it will be in five years. It is funny after just being in the USA which now has a president who tweets to the masses as his main method of communication. I know as Cuba grows as a tourist destination that the availability of Wifi will come and so will more change. I suppose they are still sorting through everything after the death of Fidel Castro and politically everything is still up in the air.

After a while I got used to it and loved the fact that I wasn't distracted by work – it actually became a really good holiday! I saw Churches everywhere; it seemed Christian people were allowed to practise openly and were not suppressed. This was another surprise!

* * *

The Malecón in the evening. A great place to go for a stroll, see classic cars, and enjoy the Havana vibes.

Photo by Antônio Milena in Wikimedia Commons, CC-BY-3.0 br.

I paid a visit to some of the local art museums. I love art museums and have visited them all over the world, so of course I had to see some in Cuba. There are several in Havana alone including the Museo de Arte Colonial and the National Museum of Fine Arts, which is in two parts, one showing international art and the other showing Cuban art.

Another place to go in Havana was the Revolutionary Museum. It was all about the Cuban Revolution and the history surrounding Fidel Castro. I found the Revolutionary Museum very enthralling; it also explained where and why the revolution took place. The museum was not just about Fidel but revolutionaries before him – which beforehand I had known little about. Ironically enough the premises of the museum consist of the former presidential palace, which looks highly conservative and traditional!

The main subject of the museum was, of course, Fidel Castro, a revolutionary who along with his brother Raúl Castro and backed by a number of Cuban revolutionaries overthrew the Batista government in 1959. In 1953, the Castros led roughly 135 men to take over the Moncada Barracks in the southern city of Santiago de Cuba, in the large, mountainous southern and eastern province of Oriente, the same Santiago where the Spanish surrendered in 1898. Extending from the Sierra Maestra to Guantánamo and Baracoa, Oriente was the historic cradle of past insurrection and independence struggle in Cuba. Unfortunately, the attack on the Moncada barracks turned out to be a failure and the would-be revolutionaries were all caught.

Many of the people who took part in this expedition were shot in the immediate aftermath. The Castros managed to escape this fate though they were among the ringleaders. Their father Angel was a prominent and well-connected member of the pre-revolutionary Cuban Establishment, and he was able to get the Roman Catholic church to intercede. Noting that Raúl

The conservative-looking Museum of the Revolution (a fragment of Havana's old city wall is also visible at the right, by the white car)

had been picked up along with Fidel, Angel said that he knew one of his sons was crazy, but hadn't realised the other one was too. The museum doesn't mention this part of the background to the story, as far as I can tell.

Instead, Fidel Castro was sentenced to fifteen years' imprisonment and Raúl to thirteen. Less than two years later, Batista freed the Castros and the other imprisoned rebels, in response to public pressure. Feeling that they were still in danger, the Castros fled into exile. In Mexico, they met fellow revolutionary, Ernesto 'Che' Guevara, an Argentinian medical doctor who had lately been in Guatemala, and decided to try and overthrow Batista again. On 25 November 1956, they sailed for Cuba with 79 other followers on board a seriously overcrowded pleasure-yacht called the *Granma*, headed for the mountainous southern Oriente province of Cuba, the cradle of past uprisings and, they hoped, the next one.

Cuba would later be divided up into a larger number of provinces. The part of the former Oriente where the Castro expedition made landfall in 1956 would be renamed *Granma*, after the boat. As to the name, the *Granma*'s original owner was an American who had apparently named it in honour of his grandma, leaving out the 'd'.

Celia Sánchez, a female hero of the revolution who been in charge of things inside Cuba while the Castros were in prison and in exile, was waiting for the boat with fifty men, trucks and other equipment. However, the *Granma* was spotted at sea and was forced to make landfall on 2 December at a less favourable location where no-one was waiting. Three days later, the rebels were attacked by the Batista's troops and very nearly wiped out.

Only twelve of the 82 individuals on the *Granma* made it to the Sierra Maestra. Those who slipped through the Batista cordon included the Castros, whom the Pope himself probably could not have got off if they had been captured again, and Guevara. The doughty twelve trained replacements and built up their following again.

Eventually Castro gained the upper hand and became the effective ruler of Cuba on New Year's Day, 1959. Almost to the very end the Batista regime hadn't really taken the rebels particularly seriously. And to make matters worse for Batista the USA imposed an arms embargo on its former ally just at the time when the fighting grew hot, deciding that this was an opportune moment to punish him for a dodgy human rights record. As such, and in a way that would soon come to appear deeply paradoxical, the Americans helped Castro into power.

At first, the Americans were well-disposed toward Castro, who toured the USA after the revolution. But as we have seen, things soon turned sour.

Ferocious warfare also raged between the new regime and remnant Batista supporters until 1965, a bloodier conflict than the revolution itself and a period of time in which most of the shootings carried out by the Castro regime itself took place. The fighting was centred on the Escambray mountains south-east of Havana, another area favourable to guerrilla activities.

This post-revolutionary civil war is not well known outside Cuba. But it explains quite a lot about the character of the regime, including the consolidation of dictatorship and the militarisation of Cuba.

It was in during the hottest period of the Escambray conflict, in 1961, that the United States organised an attack in which boatloads of exiles came ashore at the Bahía de Cochinos (Bay of Pigs), close to the Escambray range.

The Americans must have imagined that if landing a band of guerrillas close to some rugged area of Cuba had worked for the Castros – eventually – and for that matter in Guatemala, where the army stayed in its barracks, it might work for anti-Castro forces too. It didn't.

The armed forces that the Castroites put into the Escambray, amounting to hundreds of thousands of troops, liberally supplied by the Soviet Union, were a lot more powerful than Batista's small and under-equipped armed forces had been; and a lot wiser to guerilla warfare as well. At the peak of the Escambray conflict the Cuban government was able to call on a quarter of a million troops to almost literally trample out the insurgency. Why the CIA thought another 1,400 would tip the balance, or cause the Cuban army to give up, is almost unfathomable and seems to reflect some kind of a 'well, it worked last time' mentality. The situation in Guatemala had been completely different, the local army neutralised in advance, which wasn't the case in Cuba. All that the Bay of Pigs invasion succeeded in achieving, along with the Escambray insurrection, was to bolster the position of hard-liners in the Cuban regime who took the view that power grows out of the barrel of a gun.

In the first three months of 1962 General Lyman Lemnitzer, Chairman of the US Joint Chiefs of Staff, who along with the hard-line Air Force commander Curtis Le May might have been a model for the unstable generals portrayed in the classic films *Doctor Strangelove* (1963) and *Seven Days in May* (1964) – World War II veterans who seemed to regard World War III with the Communists as a more or less inevitable follow up, and nuclear weapons as just another option for fighting it – drew up a new plan for a formal US invasion of Cuba called Operation Northwoods.

Lemnitzer's plan opened with a scandalous deception campaign intended to make it look as though Cuba had attacked the United States first. The *ruse de guerre* is familiar to the military mind of course; but it is infinitely more questionable in a peacetime, political context, quite apart from the nature of the actions proposed, most of which seemed to consist of real or simulated acts of terrorism that were to be blamed on the Cubans. The original Spanish-American war had begun with the convenient but still-unexplained explosion of the USS Maine in Havana harbour, an explosion which was probably an accident. Why don't we take more definite steps to make sure that something like that happens all over again, Lemnitzer asked, even suggesting rather unimaginatively that Guantánamo Bay might be a suitable location for a re-run of the Maine incident, albeit only with fake casualties this time.

Lemnitzer followed up this overture – a good example of what that official said about how Cuba always seemed to bring out the "werewolf" in the Americans – with an invasion plan that was more realistic than the Bay of Pigs from a military point of view. Assuming from the outset that the Cubans were now fully primed and ready to fight back, any future invasion needed to be a full-on amphibious undertaking of the World War II variety, with casualties to match. Assuming everything went according to plan, the planners estimated that the American invasion force would suffer more than eighteen thousand casualties. The scale of the operation explained why it was now so important to soften up the US public and world opinion beforehand with various ruses. After only three days President Kennedy shelved the plan and made it clear that he did not think an overt invasion of Cuba would ever be put into effect.

In the meantime, an embattled Cuba became an increasingly loyal and dependent ally of the Soviet Union, which also agreed to purchase Cuban sugar, the country's chief export, at a high price. Worried about future invasion, Cuba lobbied the Soviet Union for nuclear missiles to be installed, and the Soviets agreed, viewing Cuba as a sort of unsinkable aircraft carrier and missile base just off the coast of the USA.

This led to an even greater crisis, the Cuban Missile Crisis of October 1962; after which, relations between Cuba and the USA *really* went into freefall. No other Communist country, not even North Korea, would be subjected to the kinds of unyielding sanctions that the USA have imposed on Cuba right down to the present day.

The most dangerous fact about the Cuban missile crisis was the Americans failed to realise that the Soviets had installed tactical or battlefield nuclear weapons in Cuba and that these were operational, in addition to the half-assembled strategic missiles aimed at the USA.

Thinking that they faced a last chance to stop the strategic missiles from becoming live, many in the American administration urged a surprise attack to destroy the installations, not realising that the true situation. Lemnitzer's invasion plan was also on the table. Had Kennedy changed his mind and approved any such schemes, at a minimum, it is quite likely that the American base at Guantanamo would have been wiped out by Soviet / Cuban tactical nuclear weapons already pre-positioned for that purpose.

Fortunately, attack-Cuba options were not pursued, and the crisis was resolved by means of a secret deal under which the Soviets removed their strategic missiles from Cuba, and that as a *quid pro quo* the Americans would remove some nuclear missiles they had recently installed in Turkey. To forestall any future crisis the Soviets removed the tactical weapons as well, even though the Americans never found out about them until much later.

(The American missiles in Turkey had been the original source of the crisis. The Soviets decided that if the Americans could put nuclear missiles aimed at them in Turkey, they would put similar weapons aimed at the Americans in Cuba. The whole thing was a playground exercise which soon got out of hand, the Americans conceding privately that the Soviets had a point and that in any case it did not matter very much what direction a nuclear missile came from, but not wishing to be seen to back down.)

In economic policy, Castro limited the private land people could own and largely eradicated private Cuban businesses; upheavals which led to the emigration of the two million Cubans to the US, many of them taking up residence in Miami.

In 2008 Fidel Castro resigned and gave presidency to his brother Raúl. For the people left in Cuba he is a hero and the museum show's Fidel in a positive light. I had to admire the military skills of Fidel Castro (who I also thought was quite a good-looking man!), although I hope Cuba and the world never get that close to war again!

Anyway, I met a woman from Namibia in the museum and she was an interesting lady. We talked about the revolution and how when the Soviet Union collapsed it put a lot of pressure on the government because the Soviet connection was its main source of income. She told me she had come to see the museum and Cuba – the home of Fidel – to show thanks for what he did.

Unbeknown to me Castro had a huge following in places like Namibia because he 'saved them'. Cuba under Castro had a huge army, well trained, and Castro would send soldiers to places in need. Namibia was one of these places; Castro sent soldiers to support Namibian freedom fighters against the South African government who sought to control Namibia. Castro evidentially helped gain Namibia independence. When Castro died the president of Namibia declared a three-day mourning period.

So here was this woman some distance from her home, coming here specifically to see the history of her people and pay tribute to Fidel Castro.

The museum offered a pro-revolution ideology. It showed everything good Castro's leadership gave Cuba. He gave the people education and rates of literacy approaching 100 per cent. He made changes to health care so that it was readily available and affordable to everyone no matter their background. That was admirable. He initiated the food packages given to everyone by the government so that no-one would ever have to go hungry. So, while there are some areas of poverty – they are at the very least well fed and are given medical care.

* * *

Cuba was first 'discovered' by Christopher Columbus in 1492, soon after he had made landfall on the neighbouring island that was to become known as Hispaniola. I put 'discovered' in quotes, for of course there were people living there already. Columbus is generally thought to have made his Cuban landfall at Bariay Bay toward the eastern end of Cuba's north coast. People in the nearby city of Baracoa, the first Spanish city founded in Cuba (in 1511, a few years before Havana) told me about a wooden cross that Columbus erected when he arrived. Amazingly, it still survives, the first and only survivor of 29 such crosses that Columbus erected in the course of his exploration of Cuba, and is preserved in the local cathedral, Our Lady of the Assumption.

Cuba lived under Spanish rule from the early 1500s until the end of the 1800s, becoming the world's largest producer of sugar. At the beginning of this period, the Spanish enslaved the indigenous Taíno. It wasn't long, however, before these indigenous peoples had been almost completely wiped out both physically and as a culture by European diseases, disruption of their agricultural systems and intermarriage of the survivors with Europeans, the descendants brought up in ways that were assimilated to Spanish culture. Thereafter, Africans would be brought over to be the slaves.

I learned about Cuba's strong ties with Louisiana when I was in Florida, itself under Spanish rule for hundreds of years and treated as part of Cuba for administrative purposes in those days. Modern Louisiana, and indeed much of the Mississippi region, came under Spanish control for forty years at a time when the colonisation of America was advancing rapidly, from 1762 until 1802. This large area had previously been French, and was again French briefly, until its acquisition by the USA in 1803.

Many Cubans settled in what is now Louisiana in the eighteenth and nineteenth centuries; their descendants were cut off from Cubans in Cuba during the embargo. Before Castro's revolution, New Orleans was the number-one port in the USA for the Cuban trade, and suffered from the embargo itself. Today there is strong public support for ending the embargo in Louisiana, and among Louisiana politicians of both main parties: a rather different attitude to the still-firm support shown for a continued embargo among post-revolutionary Cuban exiles in Miami.

* * *

Before I knew it, it was New Year's Eve! I was excited to see how Cubans celebrated. Well let me tell you it sure comes alive – the melodic tunes of salsa beats were everywhere, salsa on the streets and salsa in the houses! It was amazing!

I was booked in at the Inglaterra Hotel in Havana for the remainder of my time and that is where I met another three women who were travelling around Cuba. One was named Liz, a cleaner from Bermuda. Ava was a young woman from Argentina and the other was Tupia from Brisbane, Australia.

At the hotel, they had bands that would play all day, every day. Guests could buy their albums from them at the hotel. One band had about 30 members, and they were brilliant!

On New Year's Eve we went everywhere! My hotel had a five-piece band lined up for the night so I caught a few songs before I went out. In Cuba it is a tradition to have barbecued pigs on the street for New Year's. There were indeed barbecued pigs everywhere on the streets of Havana that night.

By three in the morning I was dancing on the streets. Everyone was out and really enjoying themselves. I went to the hotel Florida to get some extra salsa music in. Everyone was dancing and I was just dancing with everyone. I didn't even drink very much! It was an amazing New Year's Eve and I really enjoyed it.

Walking back to my hotel I discovered the hilarious custom pouring water out of windows onto unsuspecting passers-by, a New Year's Eve tradition apparently. I welcomed the frequent, erratic dousings of fresh water. It was hot and humid and I don't think any of us minded. So, long as no one was holding their cell phone or expensive camera, it was great!

One thing I had noticed on New Year's Eve was how well behaved everyone was – it seemed to be the police had a lot to do with that.

So, I said a happy goodbye to 2016 and welcomed in the New Year salsa dancing and having a great time!

While I was staying at the hotel I also met a guy called Rudy from Belgium. He had been going to Havana from over fifteen years. He told me how much he had noticed the prices going up in the last few years with one of the apartments in the hotel costing $400 a night.

We discussed the increase in Airbnb uptake, and the rising room rates that resulted from this.

* * *

Another great night out led me to the Buena Vista Social Club. I wanted to go somewhere I could dance and just have a good time really. I went to the Buena Vista Social Club in Marianao, a popular and touristy suburb of Havana which has long been an important entertainment district.

The original Buena Vista Social Club was a membership-only musical club in Marinao, which had enjoyed its heyday in the 1930s and 1940s and was closed in a wave of puritanism shortly after the Castro regime came to power. The club had regularly held dances and live music nights, and was the platform for local musicians to showcase their talents. The club was run as a community cofradía or a guild, based on those from the Spanish Colonial days. More specifically the Buena Vista was a 'Cabildo', meaning an African ethnic-style club. Cabildos were used as sources of entertainment and as places where ethnic Africans could celebrate and dance during holidays or festival days.

In the 1990s, some of the old performers got together with the American musician Ry Cooder to form a modern-day band called the Buena Vista Social Club, which recorded a 1997 album and became the subject of a film released in 1999, both called *Buena Vista Social Club*. Nowadays the Buena Vista Social Club, the band, is purely for tourist entertainment, something I would recommend while you're in Havana at least once in your lifetime! The beats soon had everyone up and attempting salsa dancing. I love music and dancing; the all-male trio sang beautiful songs in English and Cuban Spanish. They were accompanied by some talented dancers that even got up and did the conga line at one point. All in all, it was funny, lively and great entertainment for the beginning of the night.

A week after New Year's, the streets in Havana began to clear and the tourists began to empty the area.

On my final night of my five days in Havana I went out with Mikalena, her mother and her friend where I shouted them for a drink to say thank you. We ended up at a small bar down the road and had beer in these huge big glasses with handles. I only had one beer as I was feeling a little under the weather, but we all had a brilliant night and lots of laughs.

CHAPTER FOUR

The National Parks of Cuba

I decided that I wouldn't mind going trekking. I had planned to visit Viñales, a small town 179 kms from Havana Central. Apparently, it was the place to go for salsa dancing lessons and I thought that would have been a great experience. Viñales was a beautiful place, really dramatic scenery inland from the coast.

Viñales Valley. Baldo Simone, Wikimedia Commons, CC-BY-4.0

Viñales was popular for rock climbing and other outdoor activities – a destination frequented by tourists because it is not far from Havana. So, if that is your thing head there, you won't be disappointed.

Viñales was a beautiful introduction to the more rural areas of Cuba, a taste of what was to come. The scenery in Viñales is a combination of limestone cliff faces and tobacco plantations set amongst the Sierra de los

Órganos mountain ranges and the Parque Nacional Viñales. There is a well-known karst valley in the area – karst is the scientific name for jagged and scenic limestone country – and it was put on the UNESCO World Heritage list in 1999. And so I was all set to swap my high heels for a spot of trekking.

While I was in Havana though, I heard how it was swamped with tourists at the time, going on horse treks of all things. The local hawkers had heard and so were a bit of a problem up there. I decided I really wanted to avoid them.

I had met some other people around Havana who had travelled to Viñales just to get some private salsa lessons. I thought that would have been my cup of tea, but then they also warned me how busy it was – busier then Havana even. A smaller space with just as many tourists: stuff that, I thought.

Anyway, I passed up on the idea of going to Viñales in the end. I wanted to go the quieter parts of Cuba, the real Cuba. But perhaps I should have gone because Viñales was a famous and scenic national park

In fact, there are over forty conservation areas in Cuba, a country that takes conservation seriously, including thirteen national parks; there are nine UNESCO World Heritage sites and six UNESCO World Heritage biosphere reserves. The national parks on the mainland number the following:

- Alejandro de Humboldt
- Caguanes
- Desembarco del Granma ('Disembarcation of the *Granma*')
- Guanahacabibes Peninsula
- La Bayamesa
- La Mensura – Pilotos
- Sierra Cristal
- Sierra Maestra / Turquino
- Viñales

Viñales and Guanahacabibes Peninsula National Parks are in the west of Cuba, west of Havana. The Guanahacabibes National Park honours a people called the Guanahatabey or Guanahacabibe who inhabited the extreme far west of Cuba, where a thin peninsula juts out far into the ocean.

Moving on, Caguanes National Park is on the central part of the northern coast east of Havana. The remaining six national parks in the list just given are all in the extreme southern part of Cuba near the towns of Bayamo, Santiago de Cuba and Baracoa.

The main island of Cuba is surrounded by reefs and offshore islands. Of the national parks on the main island, it is worth noting that Guanahacabibes Peninsula National Park also has a significant offshore element. Several entirely offshore areas are also counted as national parks. These are:

- Cayos Avalos Antiles Rosario
- Jardines de la Reina ('Gardens of the Queen')
- Punta Frances
- San Felipe – Los Indios

Cuba also boasts nine UNESCO World Heritage sites:

- Alejandro de Humboldt National Park
- Archaeological landscape of the first coffee plantations in the southeast of Cuba
- Desembarco del Granma National Park
- Historic centre of Camagüey
- Old Havana and its fortification system
- San Pedro de la Roca Castle, Santiago de Cuba
- Trinidad and the Valle de los Ingenios
- Urban historic centre of Cienfuegos
- Viñales Valley

There are also six UNESCO biosphere reserves in Cuba, these being:

- Bacanoa
- Buenavista
- Ciénaga de Zapata ('Zapata Swamp')
- Cuchillas del Toa ('Ridges of Toa')
- Peninsula de Guanahacabibes
- Sierra del Rosario

CHAPTER FIVE

Varadero

ONE OF MANY CUBAN BEACHES

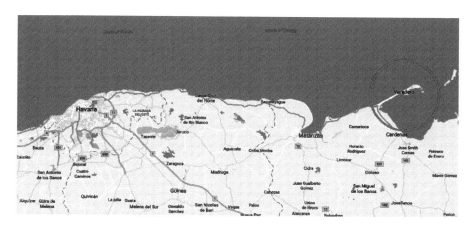

Varadero, east of Havana. Map data ©2017 Google, INEGI

Y next stop was Varadero Beach, East of Havana, and is made famous by its twenty kilometre-long spit that tourists love to hang out on. Varadero is a popular resort town and while I'm not a huge fan of these highly-condensed tourist areas, I wanted to go and see the beaches up there. I had heard they were the most beautiful white sandy beaches with turquoise waves that steadily rolled onto the shore. Varadero, I learned, also had some of the best Rumba music clubs.

I had met a woman in Havana called Ava who was from Argentina. She told me that she wanted to travel with me and we would go to a national park around that area, but it proved to be very difficult.

I had bought my bus ticket from the hotel I stayed at in Havana, and I was traveling with the main bus company Viazul. The day we were travelling the revolution was being honoured, so there was a danger of a hold-up, but my bus left early and only took two hours to get to Varadero. So east I headed by bus, all crammed in like sardines I sat back and enjoyed the scenery whizzing by for two hours. The bus Ava caught took seven hours however because of celebrations that blocked the way.

Varadero Beach is a popular tourist area not far from Havana.

Satellite image is NASA World Wind Globe v. 1.4, via ILA-boy on Wikimedia Commons. Slightly trimmed.

*Revolutionary Wall Art in Varadero the guerillero with the cowboy
hat is Camilo Cienfuegos. A notice on the door next to Camilo
advertises a function to commemorate the anniversary of the
revolution, which also falls on New Year's Day.*

'Revolution is a sense of the historical moment', a quote from a speech by Fidel Castro. Also, eating hamburgers with the locals and an incongruously un-PC statuette. All in a less touristy part of Varadero.

The much more touristy side of Varadero

Varadero is small in comparison to Havana, with a regular population of just under 28,000 people. It has the largest resort in Cuba and relies solely on resort styled accommodation to bring in the numbers of tourists which almost double the population at busy times.

For such a small town there were a vast number of hotels, over fifty I believe. That coupled with the usual tourist water activities and live poolside entertainment made it a very busy place indeed. It was a surprise to find such a busy, active area after travelling along dusty uninhabited roads to get there.

When I arrived in Varadero, I found out that my casa particular was full, but because I was friendly - although they didn't speak any English - and showed them photos of Mikalena and I on New Year's, they let me stay. It was a challenge but a great experience communicating through sign language with them. People were coming in after me and giving them money to sleep on mattresses on the floor!

The beautiful Varadero Beach in the daytime, and at sunset.
Daytime image is on Pixabay, by majkohp, CC0 public domain

The woman running it had her father working there too. He was lovely and had a dog that would follow him around. I kept meeting lovely people in Cuba. They only charged me $15 for the night. I walked into town - it was a twenty-minute walk just to get public Wifi.

I spent the day just enjoying the seaside air and tried out a few of the eateries along the main road that ran beside the beach. I wandered out to the spit but didn't walk all the way out as it was a lot further than I had thought and I worried I would get stuck out there if the tide changed. In reality, it is developed all the way out to the end, so I doubt that that is an issue in most places.

I eventually met up with Ava and we went to a restaurant where all the locals were eating. That turned out to be one of the best ideas we had! Ava ordered a vegetarian hamburger with an egg and a coffee; they charged us in the local currency so it worked out Ava paid the equivalent of twenty-five cents (US) for her meal. I learned very quickly how delicious the local food was and made a promise to eat at them more often.

Varadero was the beginning of my real Cuban holiday, even if it started off at the most popular resort town! Actually, the main reason Varadero is so popular is because it's close to Havana. I later found that Cuba has beautiful white sand beaches for most of the way around. However, many provincial parts of Cuba are well off the tourist track, so they don't get the same attention from beach lovers as Varadero.

The giveaway is the number of places on the shores of Cuba called Playa, which means beach. Clockwise on the main island of Cuba and its immediate offshore barrier islands from Cabo de san Antonio on the island's western tip, a list of localities named Playa or in one case, Cajio Beach, is as follows. I have also added the names of some other well-known cities and

Palm Trees in Varadero. Photograph by Dinkum, Wikimedia
Commons, public domain CC0 1.0, dated 4 March 2007.

capes and other localities in bold to indicate between which of these the
Playas and Cajio Beach are to be found:

Cabo de San Antonio; Playa Colorada; Playa de Cayo Jutias; Playa
Carenero; Playa Baracoa; **Havana**; Playa Jibacoa; **Varadero**; Playa El
Salto; Playa Ganuza; Playa Uvero; Playa Piñon; Playo Cayo Santa Maria;
Playa Victoria; Playa Jiguey; Playa Santa Lucia; Playa Los Piños; Playa
Covarrubias; Playa la Boca; Playa la Herradura; Playa Blanca; Playa
Pesquero; Playa Yaraguanal; Playa de Morales; Playa Juan Vicente; Playa
Corinthia; **Baracoa**; Playa de las Personas; Playa Uvero; **Guantánamo Bay**;
Playa del Este; Playa Caletoncito; Playa Cazonal; Playa de Sigua; Playa de
La Hacienda El Indio; Playa Daiquiri; Playa Damajebayo; Playa Juraguá;
Playa del Resort Bucanero; Playa Sardinero; Playa Aguadores; **Santiago**

de Cuba; Playa de Mar Verde; Playa de Caletón Blanco; Playa Asseradero; Playa Las Colaradas; Playa Habanero; Playa de las Personas; Playa Ancon; Playa Fria; Playa Ingles; Playa la Tatagua; Playa Bocanguila; Playa El Gusta; Playa Rancho Luna; Playita Junco Sur; Playa de Reina, in **Cienfuegos**; Playa Maceo; Playa Girón; Playa Larga; Playa el Rosario; Playa Mayabeque; Cajio Beach; Playa Majana; **Cabo de San Antonio**.

The Playa Daiquiri is an interesting one; it, or the locality in which it finds itself, is what the cocktail named Daiquiri named after: a name that dates back to the Spanish-American War. Daiquiri is a drink that first gained popularity among American officers stationed in the locality from 1898 onward. The recipe is essentially the same as the old Royal Navy 'grog' – that is to say rum, sugar, citrus juice to prevent scurvy, and water and/or ice – but with the distinction that a white rum such as Bacardi is necessary to make a real Daquiri, in which the subtle citrus elements are not concealed by the treacle colour (and for that matter the treacly flavours) of old-fashioned sailor rum. It just so happened that a local firm called Bacardi was brewing a white rum in nearby Santiago de Cuba and that's the connection. I don't think many people outside of Cuba had ever heard of white rum before 1898; and Daiquiris soon became fashionable worldwide in ways that Navy grog had never been. It's an ill wind that blows no good, and that was certainly the case for Bacardi, which made Puerto Rico its headquarters after Castro came to power.

Anyway, I was going to make this a bullet-pointed list, but it would have been too long. As it is, the list is not exhaustive. The more you zoom in the more Playas you find: but I wasn't going to be examining Cuba 100 metres at a time. And of course, there are other places with good beaches that aren't called Playa, or Beach: Varadero is one of them.

CHAPTER SIX
Cienfuegos

THE PEARL OF THE SOUTH

Cienfuegos, on the south-central coast of Cuba.
Map Data ©2017 Google, INEGI

AVA and I stayed for one night in Varadero, which for me was enough. Next stop was Cienfuegos, 187 km away and on the other side of the country.

My first attempt to get a bus to Cienfuegos didn't go so well. I went the day before the bus left to actually book the bus; then I would have to return on the day it departed again, to pay for it.

The first part went fine. The bus was to be leaving at 7.30 am. The following morning at 6.30am I arrived at the bus stop, to find the line out the door and down the street of the ticket booth.

One of the bus drivers was walking along talking to people while they waited and I called him over. I asked him how much the bus ride would cost and he said, $15. He pointed to a few taxi drivers milling around and said they can take you for $20. He knew of some other people wanting to go to Cienfuegos and they were all going to go in a taxi together, so they'd have room for one more. That was perfect – Ava had decided to stay in Varadero for a while longer anyway so it would just be me, myself and I going.

I ended up in a jeep-style taxi with a couple from Argentina and two guys from Mexico. The taxi driver spoke English and the trip was really nice. We stopped off along the way and had coffee and talked.

I asked the taxi driver how you could tell whether the land was privately or collectively owned. He pointed out the small patches of vegetables growing in the vast fields along the way. Those ones were privately owned, he said; the larger mass fields were the ones owned by the government. A lot of people would grow vegetables and herbs in their small patches of land, a bit extra to feed their families with.

A Restaurant and Hotel on the waterfront marina at Cienfuegos

The almost three-hour car ride to Cienfuegos actually went by really fast and before I knew it we were there careening through the streets to the casa.

I could immediately see why it's referred to as la Perla del Sur, 'The Pearl of the South'. Cienfuegos sits in a protected bay on the southern coastline of Cuba. Cienfuegos was great. The city itself was picturesque and I could immediately see the effects of tourism. It was busy! I remember getting out of the taxi feeling a little disappointed because I was hoping for something a little rural and less touristy. That's okay I was sure going to make the most of my time there anyway.

The buildings were what got me there. They were amazing, white-washed along with the typical Havana pastel colours with the old fashioned classic cars parked out the front – it was alluring.

Cienfuegos has a population of about 150,000 – the rest are tourists! It is a little bit more laid back then Varadero, with tree lined streets. A magnificent fortress sits to one side of the Cienfuegos Bay, the Castillo de Nuestra Señora de los Ángeles de Jagua built in 1745 to protect the bay from Caribbean pirates and looters.

Cienfuegos has been added to the UNESCO World Heritage list, because its buildings showcase some of the best examples of urban planning by the Spanish in the 19th century, the Spanish Enlightenment implementation.

Beyond its buildings, Cienfuegos produced a few famous personalities too, such as Benny More the Cuban singer and some other talented artists.

The city was founded in 1819 by French settlers, under the name of Fernandina de Jagua. It soon acquired the name of the Spanish Captain-General (Governor) of Cuba from 1816 until 1819, José Cienfuegos. So, it is not named after the more modern Castroite revolutionary, Camilo Cienfuegos. It officially became a city in 1880.

Cienfuegos was a strategic location for early settlers, because of the easy trading routes to Jamaica and Central and South America. In view of that, it's perhaps a little surprising that the town took so long to be founded in terms of the timeline of Spanish colonial history in Cuba, which stretches back to 1492.

I was staying at another casa lined up by Carlos from Havana, but this one actually turned out to be a room through Airbnb. They hassled me a little about not booking online and I wasn't really sure what that was about.

The service there was really good and overall Airbnb is a good choice to use in Cuba. It is becoming more and more common there. It's good because you can also read the reviews from people, so you know what ones to be wary of.

Town Hall, Cienfuegos. CC0 public domain image from Piviso.com. Architecturally rectified and cropped slightly for this book.

Central Cienfuegos, including the monument to José Martí

I had to share with another woman but she was nice enough I didn't mind. I wondered if the next time I came back if there would be more beds crammed into the rooms, which at that moment in time was pretty spacious.

Throughout the revolution and all the rest of the ups and downs of Cuban history, Cienfuegos has remained classy. Because it was founded by the French, it has a sort of New Orleans-like quality.

The natural bay that Cienfuegos encompasses adds to its decedent charm, getting it listed on the UNESCO World heritage list in 2005.

As with downtown Havana, there are three main parts that create the city, Paseo del Prado, Parque José Martí and Punta Gorda, short for Punta Gorda Cienfuegos, which is to be found on the tip of a peninsula jutting out into the almost landlocked harbour, from the city itself.

The area of Punta Gorda houses several stunning palaces with their unique French charm, I really was taken in. There was a unique French vibe to the city mixed with the usual Caribbean gleam – it felt glamorous to be honest. I was surprised because it was really laid back and everyone was friendly. Down towards the water front you can see the boats and the booming industry of shrimp farming. Cienfuegos was another prominent city in the Cuban revolution, with people protesting against the Batista government. The love of Castro and Che and the rest of the guerrillas were evident in the flags and symbols on the buildings and houses.

Cienfuegos showing location of Punta Gorda.
Imagery ©2017 TerraMetrics, Map data ©2017 Google

Punta Gorda

To the south of the city and its almost landlocked bay lies the Planta Nuclear de Juraguá, Cuba's only nuclear power plant, which was never commissioned and these days looks like a bit of a ruin.

111

Palacio de Valle from the environs of
the Hotel Jagua, Punta Gorda

I walked around not entirely sure of what to do and ended up getting a taxi that took me to Centro Recreativo la Punta, a square by the ocean at the tip of the Punta Gorda peninsula. I sat down and ordered some food at one of the restaurants, and just enjoyed the amazing tropical sunset.

While I was there, who should wander in but a visiting American celebrity who, I'm pretty sure, was Harry Belafonte, the Calypso singer and political activist from way back (born 1927), famous for songs like 'Island in the Sun' and 'Banana Boat Song' (Day-O) and much else besides that of course, including being a close associate of Martin Luther King when the Reverend King was still alive. Belafonte is still a big hit in Cuba and was still reasonably spry when I saw him. Everyone wanted to have their picture taken with Harry.

I think Cienfuegos had some of the best food I ate in Cuba. There were a few hotels around the park, mostly communist run ones, usually pretty clean and well kept.

112

Sunset on the water, Punta Gorda

I did enjoy Cienfuegos but I was beginning to be annoyed by the proximity of the crowds, like any other touristy city it was a bit overrun and I needed to head for the hills. I had thought Cienfuegos would be a little more relaxing, somewhere to breath in the fresh air and kick back with nature a bit, but Cienfuegos wasn't.

Cienfuegos was a really nice city, though. I did enjoy my time there even if it wasn't particularly what I was after.

Before I knew it - it was time to move on.

Harry Belafonte at Punta Gorda seaside bar

CHAPTER SEVEN
Bay of Pigs

SWAMPY CRADLE OF CRISIS

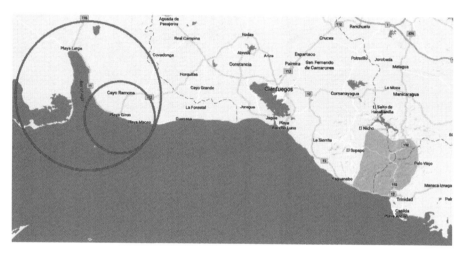

Playa Girón (small circle) and the wider Bay of Pigs area (large circle), west of Cienfuegos. Map data ©2017 Google, INEGA

I WENT down to the local non-tourist taxi stand. There were a whole lot of jeeps parked up and even though the language was a barrier I managed to organise a taxi to the Bay of Pigs.

The taxi drivers started off saying $80 for the ride, so I waited an hour and walked around for a bit. They eventually let up and I was approached by one guy who offered me a lift for $20.

The trip was 120kms to the Bay of Pigs or Bahía de Cochinos, west of Cienfuegos. The 'pigs' that the bay is named after are generally thought not to be actual pigs but a type of reef fish, *balistes vetula*, known in English as

Playa Girón, which means 'Girón Beach'.
A beautiful, palm-fringed stretch of coastline that conceals a violent past

the queen triggerfish and in Cuban Spanish as cochino – which also means pig – and probably refers to its rather fat-faced appearance.

In fact I was not headed to the bay itself but a nearby town called Playa Girón, which means Girón Beach. The town is named after a French pirate named Gilberto Giron, who in 1604 kidnapped the Bishop of Cuba for ransom and was then killed by a slave named Salvador Golomon; a story that is the subject of Cuba's first recorded literary production, *The Mirror of Patience* (1608).

The taxi ride along the coast was stunning; the scenery was enough to go there for. I notice vast areas of what looked like swamps, framed by thick jungle and bush. I had expected it to look quite dry but everything was still a dense green. All along the way there were monuments to the revolution and the soldiers who died along the way.

I got there at about ten in the morning and got out thinking, so this where the famous invasion all kicked off. It seemed so peaceful.

Playa Girón is east of the Bay of Pigs: a stunning coastal town with a stretch of blonde sand and areas of pointed rock. Playa Girón is located on an area of dry land which is effectively an island, because it is surrounded on the landward side by the one of the largest swamps in the world and the largest in the Caribbean, the Ciénaga de Zapata, which means Zapata Swamp. Designated a Wetland of International Importance under the International Convention on Wetlands, also known as the Ramsar Convention, the Ciénaga is home to many forms of wildlife. It contains large colonies of flamingos (many thousands of individuals), and many other brightly coloured species of bird inhabit the swamp and the clumps of bush in and around it as well. The Ciénaga of vital importance to North American migratory birds, and is also the chief remaining stronghold of the Cuban crocodile, said to be the world's smartest crocodile.

Like the Australian freshwater crocodile or 'freshy', the Cuban crocodile is an agile creature with some unusual characteristics. The Australian freshy and the Cuban crocodile are the only crocodile species that will run after prey on dry land and chase it down, as opposed to lunging for prey at the water's edge. Two ridges above the Cuban crocodile's eyes give it a dinosaur-like look. It can be trained to come when its name is called but not when the name of another crocodile is called; and to do tricks such as not eating food until it is told to. It is even thought to hunt in social groups that coordinate their activities. With all these characteristics some keepers refer to it, half-jokingly, as a 'velociraptor'; and although a typical specimen is not especially large, scientists are often nervous about dealing with more than one at a time.

The Cuban crocodile used to be hunted until the 1960s. It no longer faces that danger. But unless or until its numbers recover, it faces another danger, that of interbreeding with the more common American crocodile,

The Cuban Crocodile (crocodylus rhombifer).
Photograph by Zanbog, Wikimedia Commons, CC-BY-SA 2.0.

found throughout the tropical Americas, and thus getting 'bred out' in favour of a more mundane, slithery sort of crocodile: a great shame!

Playa Girón itself consists of a small jumble of ramshackle houses perched near the beach. Equipped with only a post office, grocery store and a few hotels, it's best to stock up on anything you may need before travelling here.

Playa Girón got its name from a French pirate, Gilbert Girón who lost his head when he tried to take on the locals living there. But it is best known for its unwitting part in the 1961 invasion.

Playa Girón was the main landing site of roughly 1,400 Cuban exiles who were commissioned by the American CIA (Central Intelligence Agency) to invade Cuba. The CIA was anti-Castro. They backed the remnants of Batista's forces both on the island and in exile (mostly in Miami), and with

Playa Girón Beach Scenes

A decaying sea-wall and walkway along the waterfront, Playa Girón.

the help of the exiles planned and executed an attack which would go down in history as one the greater fiascos of all time.

Under President John F. Kennedy, the exile force, called Brigade 2506, led the invasion with the main landing at Playa Girón. The site at the Bay of Pigs had been chosen for a variety of reasons, but ultimately because it was remote, almost uninhabited and considered to be a sort of 'soft underbelly' of Cuba where a moderately sizeable invasion force could come ashore without being noticed, at first.

The landing sites on the Bay of Pigs and at Playa Girón were surrounded on the landward side by the crocodile-infested Ciénaga de Zapata. The Ciénaga provided something of a defensive moat, so that the invaders could not be pushed back into the sea straight away. But by the same token, if the government army managed to block the handful of roads that crossed the Ciénaga, the invaders would probably never get to the other side of the swamp either.

So, the overall landing site wasn't really as well-chosen as all that. It was defensible, but by the very same token it was also the sort of place where the invaders could get besieged and make no further progress. And getting across the swamp was only half the battle, quite literally, as well. If the invasion force did manage to get across the Ciénaga and then ran into difficulties in the open countryside beyond, and decided that it had to join its allies in the Escambray mountains, it would have to proceed along the coast for nearly a hundred kilometres past the government-held town of Cienfuegos, while being hit sideways all the way.

It was true that the Castroites had landed with a handful of people in the 1950s, themselves. But the Castroites hadn't actually been *invading* Cuba, merely immigrating illegally with the intention of causing trouble later; and they had headed straight for the hills after stepping off the boat. And the hills had been nearby. Even then, they had been captured *en masse* the first time and taken heavy casualties the second time

No doubt some well-organised invasion force numbering in thousands, with support from battleships and aircraft carriers offshore, could have achieved the immediate objectives of the Bay of Pigs invasion. This was what the outfits such as the US Marines were good at.

But the Bay of Pigs invasion was to be a much more rickety and improvised affair than that. It would consist of 1,400 guys whose chief military qualification was that they didn't like the Castros, plus a few tanks and some obsolete aircraft. These were all to be dropped off with a handshake and "good luck." The rebels presumably also received a version of the warning soon to be made famous on *Mission Impossible*: namely, that if they were killed or captured, the secretary would disavow all knowledge of their actions. Because of course, officially, the United States didn't know anything about it. For the same reason, there wouldn't be any battleships or aircraft carriers pounding the defenders, either.

If not Mission Impossible, it was at least Mission Improbable. The scheme fell between the two stools of outright invasion and sneaking ashore to cause mischief. The government army were sure to find out, fight back, and most probably win. An officer involved in drawing up the invasion, Marine Colonel Jack Hawkins, included the phrase "this is a marginal plan"[1] in his assessment. Everything either had to go like clockwork, or degenerate into fiasco. There was no room for anything to go wrong.

And for Hawkins, that was a matter for concern. For in the best-laid plans of mice, men and marines, something usually *did* go wrong. The whole thing looked like Gallipoli all over again, except that the potential for a massacre on the beach seemed to have been even more drastically underestimated.

Pretending for the sake of argument that the scheme could succeed, the most important thing that had go like clockwork for that to even be in prospect was the destruction, on the ground, of the most dangerous elements of the Cuban air force by the aircraft available to the rebels. Those mainly consisted of a handful of World War II-vintage twin-engined bombers repainted with Cuban markings to make it look like the Cuban air force had rebelled against Castro.

These bombers were to carry out a Pearl Harbour-style sneak attack on the fighter arm of the Cuban air force and annihilate it while it was on the ground. The Cuban air force's fighter arm consisted of a mixture of early jet fighters and some Hawker Sea Furies, a propeller-driven aircraft that technically of an earlier vintage, but just as dangerous in practice.

A Sea Fury has pride of place in a museum of the Bay of Pigs invasion at Playa Girón, the Museo Girón. The last and most potent British prop

---

1 From a longer quote in Grayston L. Lynch, *Decision for Disaster: The Battle of the Bay of Pigs*, New York, Pocket Books (Simon & Schuster), 2003, ©1998 by Brassey's, at p. 115.

Hawker Sea Fury in Museo Girón.

This is a file photograph from 2006. I took several photos of this plane, but none of my photos were from quite as good an angle. It looked just the same when I was there in January 2017 including the three-colour green, blue and grey camouflage colour scheme on top, and white patch behind the left side of the engine cowling, apparently not the same as its appearance at the time of the Bay of Pigs invasion. *Photograph by Panther, Wikimedia Commons, GNFDL + CC-BY-SA.* 'A Cuban Hawker Sea Fury FB.11 fighter ("FAR 543") at the Playa Giron Museum at Matanzas, Cuba. It wears a colour scheme, not related to the original scheme used during the service years in 1958/59-1961.' Photo date 27 December 2006.

fighter of the World War II era, the aircraft was originally called the Fury, a replacement for earlier types such as the Spitfire. The Fury arrived too late to take part in World War II. But it was put into production anyway and flew off British aircraft carriers for the remainder of the 1940s and 1950s, whence the name Sea Fury. Even in 1961 this aircraft was by no means completely out of date. The Sea Fury came with a 2,480-horsepower engine, four cannon and up to twelve rockets, and very much looked the business.

Whoever controlled the air would control the roads across the Ciénaga, and would thus be in a position to ensure that the first phase of the invasion ended either in a breakout or wipeout. The rebel air force, such as it was, might be able to wreck the Sea Furies and jets if it could catch them on the ground. But if any of the latter got off the ground, the rebel aircraft would be no match in a dogfight.

"If only one of his [Castro's] fighters is left intact," wrote Colonel Hawkins, "the invasion forces must withdraw at once, otherwise, this operation will result in complete disaster."[2] Well, several government fighter aircraft *did* get off the ground, and the operation *did* end in complete disaster for the invasion forces.

Massive helpings of blame would be duly served up all over official Washington in the aftermath. How had such a crack-brained scheme ever gone ahead? The now-famous term 'groupthink' was coined by the psychologist Irving Janis to describe the process by which the invasion had come to be seen as a good idea when, patently, it hadn't been a sound plan at all.

It turned out that almost everyone who was in on the scheme had had the same sorts of doubts as Colonel Hawkins, or other ones. But, much as in the tale of the Emperor's New Clothes, hardly anyone had wanted to speak out too boldly, for fear of seeming weak and unenthusiastic compared to the others, who also bit their tongues.

Although the 1961 Bay of Pigs invasion and the 1962 Cuban Missile Crisis are two separate incidents, they are often confused in people's minds. And the

2   From the longer quote in Lynch, *Decision for Disaster*, at p. 115. Clarification in square brackets added for this book.

Bay of Pigs did set the stage for the Cuban Missile Crisis nearly a year and a half later, as the Cubans decided that they needed even more weapons to be landed – why not the big one? – while the Americans became determined to reverse their humiliation, thereby setting the scene for another crisis.

I booked into the Hotel Horizontes Playa Girón at $80 a night, which was incredibly cheap for a hotel on the beach (which is what the word 'playa' means in Spanish), and was pleased to find that this area was not over run with tourists. I met a few locals who were staying in the hotel as well, they were an interesting bunch. They told me about a crocodile farm nearby and how you could even have a crocodile meat dinner (hopefully not that of the Cuban crocodile, which is endangered). I had already visited an alligator farm in Louisiana a few weeks ago, so I didn't feel the need to visit.

I went to the Museo Girón. It was interesting because, unlike the revolutionary museum in Havana which was more political, this one was more military in character and focused on the actual Bay of Pigs invasion; though not entirely, as it also had displays about the wider Bay of Pigs region (which used to be particularly under-developed) and its wildlife, and struggles against poverty and illiteracy.

Two guys were in the museum at the same time as me. One was a teacher and I wasn't sure what the other one did, but he spoke fluent English. I asked if he minded if I went around with him and he could read everything out to me, because everything was in Spanish. It was interesting because as much as I tried to pry information out of him about his political views he didn't offer up any.

I asked him why people weren't too keen to talk about their political views. I did want to find out what people thought, to get a better understanding. He told me that they didn't want Cuba to turn in to a Miami, they wanted some changes but not a lot and for the most part they were happy. They

*Museo Girón frontage, including monument to casualties
('Martyrs of Playa Girón')*

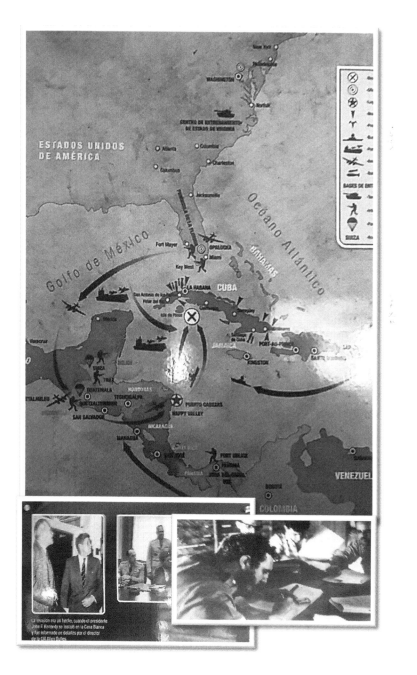

Museo Girón exhibits on the course of the Bay of Pigs invasion

loved the society they lived in and that all they simply wanted was a society that cared for its people, not a ruthless society that didn't. I understood that, maybe we can all take a leaf out of Cuba's book on that at least.

It was small and I found very simple, but it was still interesting to look at old photographs and monuments. It was then I really noticed that there were no women in any of the pictures at this museum or the one in Havana. I knew women were a big part of the revolution and a few had very prominent roles in it, but there was nothing about them. I wondered why. Possibly all this guns and ammo was a bit of guy thing, just as it is for the Americans? Celia Sánchez is commemorated in a watermark on current 5 and 10 CUP peso notes, and has her name on some public buildings and memorials, and Vilma Espin is commemorated elsewhere as well, but not so much in these museums.

The Museo Girón also showed the determination of the Cuban people. They gained independence from all the countries who tried to colonise, while Puerto Rico didn't. Cuba got its independence in the end and was well and truly better off for it, problems notwithstanding.

Going around the museum, I hadn't realised how many different areas of the country were significant in the revolution. Che Guevara was actually stationed in Havana a lot of the time, while Castro was hiding out in the Sierra Maestra Mountains. A lot of people speculated they had a falling out.

I was left in admiration of Cuba's military might; after all it is not a large country by worldwide standards.

I wandered around for a while afterward and found some nice places to eat and drink. I went for a swim in the water as the air began to warm up, and just enjoyed the tranquillity of the place. It was hard to imagine planes flying overhead dropping soldiers into the bushy areas up behind the bay and even then, the large naval ships that would have entered the bay to

Vultures nestling in Strategic Lookouts at Playa Girón

invade Cuba. It seemed too nice of a place to be spoiled by war and death. But then I suppose that's always the way. 'Behold the summer grass, all that remains of the dreams of warriors' wrote the Japanese poet Bashō.

I was walking around and I saw a vulture nesting ground, framed in the backdrop by revolutionary flags, it was quite a powerful sight. 'Behold the nesting vultures, all that remain of the dreams of warriors', Bashō might say.

Going back to the hotel I noticed how raggedy it looked, almost like it was about to fall down. Chipped stone work and cracks rendered the exterior. I asked the manager why it looked in such a state, I figured they must have a lot of tours through here and tourists in general.

129

The woman at the desk who was managing the place said, she would have loved to do the place up but because of the high taxes from the government they just didn't have the money for it. They also wanted Wi-Fi, but really everything comes down to having the money.

This was a revealing anecdote, which resonated with the familiar stories anyone who grew up in the Cold War would tend to hear about Communist economic mismanagement and hostility to entrepreneurship.

To the extent that this sort of thing is widespread, it is the other side of Cuba. It's probably not even all that different from the way things were done in China in the days of Chairman Mao – as opposed to China today.

Apart from all that, I spent a lot of time walking around and enjoying the historical significance of the place. You could do biking tours, diving and snorkelling or head to the swamp, of which the best parts are enclosed in the Parque Nacional Ciénaga de Zapata. It costs $100 for the foreign visitor to get in. I think all the national parks have some kind of entrance fee, so it can get quite pricey. I was counting my change by this stage, so I didn't go there.

I got a taxi the following day back into Cienfuegos and got straight back on a local bus to Bayamo via Trinidad.

CHAPTER EIGHT
Trinidad

GREAT ARCHITECTURE AMID RUN-DOWN AREAS

Trinidad, east of Cienfuegos. Map data ©2017 Google, INEGA

I HAD decided that I wanted to do some trekking in the Cuban mountains. I just got that itch to get out of town and the seaside resorts, and do it.

I settled on climbing the highest peak in Cuba, Pico Turquino, which had also concealed Fidel Castro's hideout on its slopes in the 1950s – why not see both? To do that meant travelling to the south of Cuba and to the southern city of Bayamo, the jumping-off point for people who wanted to climb Pico Turquino.

I figured I would go there via the city of Trinidad, east of Cienfuegos; I wanted to see as much of Cuba as I could.

Getting to Trinidad proved a bit of problem. The tourist bus services run by Viazul did not go there for some reason, so I ended up on a local bus.

The bus ride from Cienfuegos to Trinidad was only 90 kilometres, and only took an hour and a half to get there.

I was only going to be stopping off in Trinidad, so it would be a quick look around the bus station and a scenic ride through the city.

Trinidad is another coastal city and the bus ride was an attraction in itself. We bumped along the dusty road and were greeted with vast green plantations of tobacco plants and sugar cane. On the odd occasion, I got a glimpse of blue ocean in the distance. It was an amazing ride, probably one of the better ones I did.

It was real rural Cuba. I didn't see anyone working in the fields either which was interesting. Just rows and rows of sugarcane and tobacco with the rugged Escambray mountains in the backdrop. The roads were quite narrow along this stretch and we passed by a couple of white washed houses hugging close to the road side. I was amazed at the contrasting dry rocky ground and then the lush green of the fields and plantations mixed together. The fences posts were lines of tree branches, bent and uneven with wire running between them.

We drove through the streets of Trinidad towards the bus stop and I was amazed at the buildings they featured.

Trinidad was the place you really felt like time had just stopped. Everything was really well-preserved, all these stunning colonial buildings.

I did notice that there seemed to be two sides to Trinidad, one was these exquisite examples of Spanish Colonial architecture, and the other side consisted of the run-down non-tourist areas.

Trinidad: its rooftops and the bell tower of San Francisco de Asis.

An old-fashioned view of an old-fashioned town where people still lead old-fashioned lives. *Photograph by Isaychev, Wikimedia Commons CC-BY-SA-3.0-Deed, taken 5 Dec. 2008*

The Spanish colonialists developed very specific plans on the layouts of their conquered areas. The building of cities in the New World meant adhering to a very carefully laid out set of rules and patterns called La Traza.

Many of the old buildings featured similar styles, really a key feature of the city along with the people selling wares from their bicycles. I saw a number of donkeys and horse-pulled carts rambling slowly on the street. It was amazing and I really could have got lost back in time along with the buildings.

As an old-fashioned colonial town not yet affected by the automobile, Trinidad is very compact and walkable. It is only about two and a half kilometres across, yet it has a population of about seventy thousand.

Before I knew it was time to get back on the bus and travel a mind boggling 380 kilometres to Bayamo, a very long, long, seven hours further south.

We passed through other towns like Florida and Camagüey, not arriving till well into the evening at Bayamo.

Trinidad has been a thriving city since the early 1500s, when it was founded by Diego Velázquez.

Trinidad, view from the bell tower

I did notice that the seemed to be two sides to Trinidad, one was these exquisite examples of Spanish Colonial architecture, and the other side consisted of the run-down non-tourist areas.

The Spanish colonialists developed very specific plans on the layouts of their conquered areas. The building of cities in the New World meant adhering to a very carefully laid out set of rules and patterns called La Traza.

Many of the old buildings featured similar styles, really a key feature of the city along with the people selling wares from their bicycles. I saw a number of donkeys and horse-pulled carts rambling slowly on the street. It was amazing and I really could have got lost back in time along with the buildings.

As an old-fashioned colonial town not yet affected by the automobile, Trinidad is very compact and walkable. It is only about two and a half kilometres across, yet it has a population of about seventy thousand.

Before I knew it was time to get back on the bus and travel a mind boggling 380 kilometres to Bayamo, a very long, long, seven hours further south.

We passed through other towns like Florida and Camagüey, not arriving till well into the evening at Bayamo.

Painting of Trinidad de Cuba by Granville Perkins, 1874; Entrance sign to Trinidad with partial replica of the rural watchtower Torre Manacas-Iznaga (in pink); tower of San Francisco de Asis, which also appears on the CUC 25 centavo coin.

Images all in Wikimedia Commons. Painting is public domain, ex Boston Public Library (print); Iznaga tower image is by Alexandra, CC-BY-SA 3.0, taken on or before 25 May 2006; San Francisco image with coin is by Yomangani, public domain, created 1 January 2007.

*The Municipal History Museum in Trinidad, located in the
Palacio Cantero, with external views of the Palacio Cantero
observation tower from Plaza Mayor at top.*

Top image and image detail from photograph by Leon Petrosyan on
Wikimedia Commons, CC-BY-SA 3.0, taken on or before 9 December
2011. Arcchitecturally rectified and cropped for this book. Bottom
image from photograph by Gorupdebesanez, Wikimedia Commons,
CC-BY-SA 3.0, taken 24 April 2003 by camera metadata record.

137

Top Image: The Palacio Brunet, which today contains the Romantic Museum, with San Francisco de Asis tower to the left. Bottom images: street scenes with animal transport.

Top image from photograph by Nevit Dilmen, Wikimedia Commons, CC-BY-SA 3.0, dated 1 February 2017, image architecturally rectified and cropped slightly for this book. Bottom images from photographs by Arnoud Joris Maaswinkel (left), Wikimedia Commons, CC-BY-SA 4.0, dated 31 March 2015; Anagoria (right), Wikimedia Commons, CC-BY-3.0, dated 15 February 2012. Both lower images cropped moderately for this book.

Casa de la Música, Trinidad.

Top image and image detail from photograph by Leon Petrosyan on Wikimedia
Commons, CC-BY-SA 3.0, taken on or before 9 December 2011. Architecturally
rectified and cropped for this book. Scenes photographed by Yoel Díaz,
'Yoeztudioz', Wikimedia Commons, CC-BY- 3.0, all scenes dated 2 October 2016.
The Casa de la Música is a regular almost 24- hour venue, according to Díaz.

CHAPTER NINE
Bayamo

SMALL BUT FRIENDLY CITY – I LIKE IT!

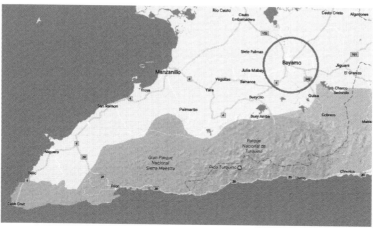

Bayamo, and its location in Cuba. Map data ©2017 Worldatlas.com
for upper map, ©2017 Google, INEGA, for lower map

I WAS quite surprised to learn that Bayamo, a city of a little over 220,000 in the south of Cuba, is older than Havana and Santiago de Cuba. Bayamo was the second city founded by Diego Velázquez in Cuba.

I was really taken with Bayamo, nicknamed the 'city of horse carts' – for there were more here than in Trinidad, really adding to its rustic antiquated charm.

My friend Carlos had organised my accommodation ahead of me arriving with his father at a casa. I had to laugh when I arrived, tired and hot because I was again told that his casa was full. He got one of the staff to take me down the road to another one, I only needed a bed for a night so I was ready to happily take whatever was available.

Even though it was late, I found myself unsettled and I needed to get out and stretch my legs so I went for a walk. The sun had well set and there were quite a few policemen around. I made my way to the main town square, Parque Céspedes. I found somewhere that had internet so I jumped on to check my emails. I noticed the policemen came and stood closer to me, until they were only a few feet away. One guy I got chatting too, who was another teacher – honestly, I met so many doctors and teachers there it was quite incredible – told me that it wasn't safe for me to be out on my own at night.

I was surprised by his warning and figured that's why I had a number of policemen gathered around me. I hadn't had a problem with this before in any of the other towns, I think the police around made me feel pretty safe though. There are curfews in place for the young people there too, which is great, and I thought would make it completely safe. I noted his warning but still wandered back to my casa on my own anyway.

Bayamo was a pleasant surprise; I would describe it as charming. There were nice buildings everywhere and there was a prominent university here. Bayamo sits inland and was a populated city in the 1500s; it gave protection

Calle General García, in Bayamo (A mostly pedestrianised street with many cafes, eateries and bars)

Photograph by Marcel601 on Wikimedia Commons, GFDL, picture taken 3 August 2012. Slightly cropped and architecturally rectified for this book.

from the Caribbean pirates who frequented the coast and the city of Santiago de Cuba to the south. It was a rich agricultural area and one of its most influential early citizens was a Basque landowner by the name of Francisco Iznaga. His descendants that famously went on be influential in Trinidad as well, and to fight in the independence wars in the mid 1800's.

Indeed, the Cuban national anthem is a stirring march called 'La Bayamesa', meaning 'the Bayamese' or 'the one from Bayamo', most probably because it was first performed during the Battle of Bayamo in 1868, a battle

143

Dry and Wet: Another section of Calle General García, in Bayamo.

Top photograph by nurzumspass on Wikimedia Commons, CC-BY-3.0, picture taken 6 March 2012 Bottom photograph by Ro1k on Wikimedia Commons, CC-BY-3.0, picture taken 15 August 2011

144

Calle General García, and cobblestoned street with cart. Note the way that the lamp-post has been made to look like a tree in the top photo!

Both photographs by Ro1k on Wikimedia Commons, CC-BY-3.0, picture taken 15 August 2011

145

A sugarcane plantation near the roadside, outside Bayamo

between Cuban freedom fighters and the Spanish army. Grammatically speaking, the title could also mean 'the girl from Bayamo'. But there is no reference to any soldiers' sweethearts in the lyrics, which have always been rather more of the warrior-monk sort:

Run to battle, people of Bayamo!

For the motherland looks proudly to you;

Do not fear a glorious death,

For to die for the motherland is to live.

Living in chains is to live

Mired in shame and disgrace,

Hear the sound of the bugle;

Run, brave ones, to battle!

To the singers of the National Hymn (named individuals) in this place, under the direction of the Maestro Manuel Muñoz Cedeño they sang for first time (officially) the National Hymn the 8 of November of 1868.'

Photograph by Giv von Koerber, Wikimedia Commons, GFDL, photograph taken 1986. Architecturally rectified and cropped (wall background only) for this book.

The name reflects the prominent place of Bayamo and the southern part of Cuba in the country's revolutions up to that point and, as it would turn out, for the next hundred years as well.

I got up early and found a taxi driver to take me to the village by Pico Turquino. Now the issue was and that I hadn't realised until I tried was that to go into the national park, you actually have to have a special license – even for taxi drivers.

You need a proper taxi driver or you just can't go. I eventually found one who drove me out there for $45. I was going to trek first to Fidel Castro's hideout in the Sierra Maestra mountains and then on another day head up to Pico Turquino, the highest peak in all of Cuba.

Anyway, I went back to my casa to get my things and the taxi driver would meet me out the front. He turned up in a cap and blasting rap music from his car. I laughed and thought who is this guy!

The taxi driver was lovely, his name was Anley and I would be sharing the ride with a British couple. I grabbed the front seat and got chatting with the taxi driver who spoke fluent English. He was a really interesting guy, and as the car wove through the lush countryside we spoke about many things.

Anley had lived all over the world. His most recent jaunt had been in Germany where he had tried to live for three months but found it a challenge and so returned to Cuba. He said the tourist industry was really just beginning to boom and at one stage, and it was he who told me how the casas particulares were born.

He told me that's how a lot of Cubans have made their money and become quite wealthy. He considered himself to be quite well off earning $6,000 a year which I thought was really good compared to the $20 a month I had been told others were earning before tips. That was one thing in Cuba I did notice. There was an income division and it was becoming more apparent, especially in the south of the country. Tourism was a booming industry: more people were coming back to Cuba to get involved and take their slice of the pie and more building was going on.

We talked about taxes and how Cubans were still adjusting to the idea of paying them. Until recently they were used to a communist government where they didn't have to pay anything at all. Nowadays the tax level on small businesses can be as high as 50%, which gives way to the elusive black market.

When the tax systems were first introduced, Anley told me, the government had expected small entrepreneurs to cough up $200 per month in some places, and that's why a lot of people left. Now that things have been adjusted and settled down somewhat, many want to come home.

Anley admitted he did live a good life compared to some in Cuba. He was a 35-year old man making a good income and for that reason he did not need to move to a bigger city, as many were.

He talked about a friend of his who had moved to the USA during this time and had to retrain for ten years to become a nurse. The challenge was the embargo and then the language barrier. Cuban doctors found it difficult to find work abroad and many had to retrain as well, it all took a lot of time and effort. Anley was quite proud of the fact that Cuban doctors had developed some excellent advances in medicines in diabetes and lung cancer treatments – they didn't have a choice because of the embargo.

I thought that was quite a big achievement for Cuba and I personally think New Zealand could have some huge benefits from trading with them.[1] I do, I think the whole world should start trading with Cuba.

Anley was from Bayamo himself and so he put us onto a government hotel. I had discovered that there is virtually one in every town and they were some of the safest places to eat at especially down this way. One thing I was extremely wary of was where I was eating; the last thing I wanted was to be cooped up in a room bed-ridden from gastro infections.

Anyway, it was a very educational taxi ride to Bayamo and in reflection, the best way to find out about the real Cuba is conversations with the locals – particularly the ones in the tourist industry. They are more open to having discussions about everything and they usually speak fluent English which makes it easier for me, not knowing the local language too well.

1   See, further, Jorge I. Dominguez, 'What you might not know about the Cuban economy', Harvard Business Review, 17 August 2015.

CHAPTER TEN
Fidel's Hideout in the Sierra Maestra

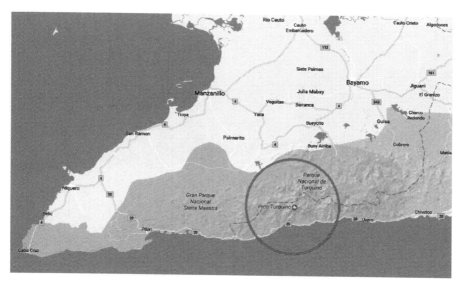

The Sierra Maestra: the village of Santo Domingo, the Comandancia de la Plata and Pico Turquino are all inside the red circle, southwest of Bayamo. Map data ©2017 Google, INEGA

B ASING myself for a time in the small mountain village of Santo Domingo in the Turquino National Park, also known as the Sierra Maestra Great National Park (Spanish: *Gran Parque Nacional Sierra Maestra*), the home of Fidel, was one of the best ideas I had while I was in Cuba.

It gave me the ability to take my time and explore the national park piece by piece.

*Santo Domingo: the mountain village, strung out along a main road, that
is the base for trips to the Comandancia de la Plata and Pico Turquino*

My first goal and adventure was to head off to see Fidel Castro's hideout, a short and mostly manageable trek for 2 hours up the mountain.

Fidel Castro's hideout was something I wanted to see because it was where he hid and built up his forces for three years after getting off the Granma – I wanted to see how and where he did that.

They called it the Comandancia de la Plata, high up in the Gran Parque Nacional Sierra Maestra and covered by dense bush and forest. It was from

The Old Castro Hideout, the 'Comandancia de la Plata', Sierra Maestra

here that Fidel conducted attacks on the rural patrols in the area and finally at Batista himself.

I had noticed that the locals seemed to hold a flame to Che Guevara more than Fidel. There were more pictures of him around in Havana and Bayamo then of Fidel, although this was probably because Che was a martyr to revolution at the comparatively young age of 39, and because Fidel wished to discourage a personality cult involving the veneration of anyone living.

Trekking (or tramping, or hiking) goes hand in hand when travelling. I love it. There is nothing like getting outdoors into the less populated areas. I love native bush and have spent a lot of time volunteering for the Department of Conservation back in New Zealand, which brought me right up close with the outdoors. I have found a new love of plants, bromeliads in particular, and an appreciation for the wildlife that flourishes in the wilderness.

The next morning, I met the group I would be trekking with, and the guide, at the park entrance.

It was a two-hour hike up the mountain side, through thick bush and trees that soared into the sky. The birdlife was amazing, the bush and forest was filled with birdsong. It was an easy enough trek, it was hot and the weather was beautiful that day!

There were all these little wooden sign posts along the way directing us where to go. When we got to the little encampment I was surprised to find a mini museum there too. It felt a little eerie wandering around what was once a full functioning camp, and I imagined all the planning, discussions, and late night escapades the men would have had while they lived here. It was from here that Fidel conducted attacks on the rural patrols in the area and finally at Batista himself. I could see how it was difficult for Batista's forces to find them or even launch an attack on the area.

It all had quite a fanatical romanticism about the place, handsome young men rebelling against a government they thought was fraught with problems. The notion and ideas of a better Cuba for the people, was quite

More images of the Comandancia and its stunning views

Fidel Castro and Celia Sánchez in exhibit, Comandancia de la Plata. The quoted passage reads thus: 'For us the place most familiar, most dear, of the decisive moments of the war, from the first combats to the last in the Sierra Maestra, was la Plata' – Fidel

The Casa de Fidel at la Comandancia de la Plata. Where better to put a souvenir Che Guevara army hat to good use?

Upper photograph taken by Anagoria, on Wikimedia Commons, CC-BY-3.0, photograph taken 19 February 2012

intriguing. It was the Cuba version of Robin Hood, giving back Cuba to the poor.

The little museum that was part of the encampment showed more photos of the revolutionaries smoking cigars, combined with images of serious discussions taking place and portraits of the men. For again, I noticed that most of the revolutionaries were men, though not in every case.

It did make me realise the substantial strength of the Cuban military under the leadership of Fidel. After Fidel was successful in his overthrowing of the Batista led government he used the area as a military training area. After the Portuguese colonial empire collapsed in 1975, Cuba sent tens of thousands of troops and other aid workers to Angola, eventually defeating the efforts of Apartheid-era South Africa to install a friendly government in Angola, and ensuring the victory of a left-wing pro-Cuban one instead. Between the middle of 1975 and 1976 the Cubans managed to install a left-wing government in Angola, chasing out the forces of the right-wing one that South Africa was backing. The Soweto riots in 1976 are thought to have been emboldened by this reversal for the white regime. The South Africans came back, however, and so did the Cubans. At the peak of its involvement in the late 1980s, Cuba had 55,000 troops in Angola, bolstering the forces of Angola's left-wing government, and at the little-known but significant Battle of Cuito Canavale in 1988, said to have been the biggest battle in Africa since World War II, the Apartheid-era South African armed forces were directly defeated and completely driven out of Angola. Was the next stop to be Pretoria?

Part of the problem for the South Africans was that their armed forces were becoming increasingly debilitated by international sanctions, whereas the Cubans had the benefit of the latest Soviet equipment. Things were going badly for the Soviets and their allies elsewhere by 1988; but things were still going their way in Angola.

The battle of Cuito Canavale and everything leading up to it is generally credited with triggering the process by which Apartheid unravelled soon afterward. After Cuito Canavale, it was clear that South Africa was in a precarious position so long as it was being squeezed between sanctions and various enraged foes, both of which would probably go away at the same time if Apartheid was ended. In fact, the Soviet Union was about go away soon whether Apartheid was ended or not. But no-one in Pretoria knew that at the time.

The history of Cuba and its wars, revolutions and interventions is quite problematic for anyone who supposes, or hopes, that military conflict is obsolete. The Cubans must surely imagine that just about everything they have got, they have got by fighting for it and not by Gandhi-like methods.

Equally, the history of South Africa is confounding for those who have a black and white view of the Cold War confrontation between the Free World and the 'Evil Empire' of the Soviets, since the mostly dictatorial Soviet Union was doing more to liberate South Africa than the free West was at this time. Sanctions had been imposed in the West thanks to grassroots Anti-Apartheid protest movements; but most Western politicians otherwise still seemed to view Apartheid South Africa as a fortress against Communism. They did not realise just how wobbly the fort's walls were and how brittle the rock on which it stood, nor did they spend too much time thinking about what it must be like to be in the dungeons.

Of course, someone getting shot in the process of trying to scramble over the Berlin Wall would not have seen the Soviet Union and its allies as the good guys. All the same, there is such a thing as being 'on the right side of events'. Thus, the Castroite Cubans and the Soviets were on the right side of events in Southern Africa even if the Soviets soon turned out to be on the wrong side of events in Europe.

In fact, being on the right side of events seems to have been a particular skill of the Castro regime. A serious blunder in the course of the Cuban revolution, or a failure to detect what way the proverbial winds of change in Africa were blowing, could have finished off the Castro faction: which has often been 'up against it' at the best of times. Yet as we have seen it has just about always been Castro's adversaries who could be relied upon to make mistakes that would let the Castroites live to fight another day (literally so, if you recall that story about how the Castro brothers were amnestied right at the start of their revolutionary career). Like the cat, Fidel Castro and Castro-ism have had nine lives, their own sharpness and the blunders of their enemies preserving them at every turn even as other Communist regimes fell.

Or more than nine lives if we add in the many lurid stories about assassination plots against Fidel Castro, some strange and incredible, many of them true. As we now know, none of these plots would ever succeed (unless they finally got to Fidel in the old-folks home and managed to make it look like natural causes). One reason the plots kept failing was because of characteristics in common with the Bay of Pigs invasion. That is, a combination of a tendency to rely on enthusiastic amateurs who'd never done this sort of thing before and a long-shot under-resourced plan, just so that it could be pretended that the USA and its well-equipped forces had nothing to do with the affair.

It would be a very long time before the Americans finally decided to give up trying to have Fidel Castro done away with by methods that obviously weren't working It has been said that as far as the Americans were concerned he was the Osama bin Laden of his day; except that for diplomatic reasons the Americans weren't allowed to send in the Seals to wipe him out and had to hope, instead, that Fidel would pick the one cigar out of the box that had poison on it, or something like that..

And yet Fidel Castro *wasn't* bin Laden: an international outlaw, wanted dead or alive by all sorts of people. As the phrase "for diplomatic reasons" suggests, Fidel Castro was not an international outlaw but the ruler of a neighbouring country! It was as if the Americans had decided that the best way to avenge some past insult by the British would be to encourage someone to knock off the Prime Minister of Canada. So, this was another characteristic that the assassination plots against Fidel Castro had in common with the Bay of Pigs affair. Namely, a somewhat crazy quality that went beyond the details to encompass the whole thing.

Fidel had a tumultuous love life, with a wife from whom he split in 1955, mistresses and a number of kids. Some became Fidel loyalists, some ended up living in the United States with their mother. The old feminist saying that 'the personal is political' applies here, I suspect.

I was little peeved with our guide, because he offered to take photos of us all in front of the hide out, which sounded like a friendly thing to do, and then charged us $5 each for doing so! Still, you can see the temptation to do so in view of the poverty of the locals and how far a few American dollars or CUC pesos go in Cuba. By pulling this stunt, in a day he could make as much as ordinary Cubans do in a month.

On the way back down the mountain ranges we stopped in at a local coffee plantation, where a woman showed us the process of making coffee. She showed us where she dried the beans and then gave us each a free cup of coffee to sample.

Everyone had spent their change on the photographs and I only had $2 to give her. She grinned from ear to ear, and I felt really sorry for her. Here was this guide taking all the money even after we had paid him for taking us up, and then there she was handing out free coffees and getting nothing.

On the way down, the guide was saying how he had a sore back and didn't think he could do the tour guiding much longer so he was trying to make as much as he could while he could. I wasn't entirely fooled by his story, I guess there must be a lot of this sort of thing happening around Cuba now. Some people get tips and others don't – yet the people rely on the extra cash to make a decent living.

I was surprised by the amount of people who let straight after the trek to go back to Havana. A lot of people come down this way into the far

A Tocororo or Cuban Trogon.

Photograph by Laura Gooch, uploaded by Snowmanradio
on Wikimedia Commons, CC-BY-SA-2.0

south to see Fidel's hideout and then head straight back to the capital city. I personally think what a waste of time: you don't come to a country and not explore it.

I do think that a lot of disinformation is circulating around, one area competing against the next for tourists and their money. Telling tourists that you can't stay in that town, or the hotels or casas are full, to keep them in their own town. It's quite interesting – the effects of tourism.

After the trek, we headed back into the little one-street mountain village of Santo Domingo at the bottom of the national park, and I checked into in a hotel. I got to stay in the room where Fidel Castro stayed when he wasn't up the mountain at the Comandancia, number six. People would take photos of the room as they walked by which was funny.

It was quite special staying in Fidel Castro's room because in fifty or sixty years nothing had changed. It still had his bed he slept in and his wooden writing desk in the corner. It was quite exhilarating to think I was actually staying in his room, a humbling and honourable experience. The kitchen where they cooked the meals provided for us was well-kept and very clean.

Hiking to the Comandancia, the bird song was beautiful. The view from room six was excellent for a nature-lover, I could see the birds in the trees and the thickness of the dense jungle out the windows. I saw the national bird, the tocororo or Cuban trogon, which has plumage in the colours of the Cuban flag: red, white and blue. I saw tiny bee hummingbirds flitting amongst the trees again, and woodpeckers! It was a living museum of wildlife.

I watched a live band perform at the hotel. They sang the song 'Guantanamera', which was so cool! The guys were on guitar and drums, singing together: it was a great atmosphere. Guantanamera was a huge hit when it was released in 1966 by the Sandpipers; it became the most well-

Guantanamera

Chorus:

Guantanamera, guajira guantanamera.
Guantanamera, guajira, guantanamera

I am a truthful man, come from where the palm tree grows,
I am a truehearted man, who comes from where the palm trees
grow,
Before I lay down my life, I long to coin the verses of my soul.

Chorus

I plant a snowy rose in January and July,
I grow a snowy rose in January and July,
For the open-hearted friend who puts a helping hand in mine.

Chorus

The words that I write are radiant crimson and emerald bright,
The poems that I write are radiant crimson and emerald bright,
My verses are a wounded deer seeking shelter in the mountain
height.

Chorus

known Cuban song internationally. It is also famous in Cuba with a patriotic reason to it, the band crafted lyrics taken from a poem written by José Martí, the revolutionist. The title refers to a country girl or peasant woman from the town of Guantánamo, the 'guajira Guantanamera' that is the song's most familiar refrain. It's one those classic songs that you just want to get up and get your groove on to.

The song is generally thought to date back to the 1920s and to have been composed, with non-political lyrics at that time, by a popular radio show host called Joseíto Fernández. Sometime later, another Cuban-born composer, Julián Orbón, blended in some patriotic poetry by José Martí, thus creating what is called the 'definitive' version of the song, the one that is most familiar today. Guantanamera was popularised among non-Cuban audiences for the first time by the left-wing American folk musician Pete Seeger, who performed the Orbón version, with some of the lyrics in English, as a peace anthem in 1963: a time when Cuba was on everybody's mind because of the recent Cuban missile crisis.[1]

After that, the half-in-English Seeger version was picked up by the Sandpipers and also performed by the fabulous Joan Baez, a prominent folksinger from the USA, who also created a version of the song. I love both versions of the songs. The song is in Spanish but there is also an English translation and the lyrics are deep and meaningful. Joan Baez was also an activist and heavily involved in the civil rights movement, at the time.

The following morning, I passed through the small village once more to go on my next trek to the summit of Pico Turquino. I noticed the houses with their doors already swung open to let in the cooler air, had dirt floors. I recognized one of the guitarists from the band who had played the night before in my hotel sitting inside one of them. That made me feel a little sad, it was my first sighting of real poverty in Cuba.

---

1   David Cheal, 'The life of a song: "Guantanamera"', Financial Times, 14 March 2015.

CHAPTER ELEVEN
Pico Turquino

THE HIGHEST PEAK IN CUBA

Pico Turquino, showing rare snowfall.
Photograph originally uploaded 9 April 2011 by Cuba4 on Panoramio, attribution share-alike.

Pico Turquino is the highest point in all of Cuba. It is only 1,974 metres high, but the dramatic scenery is in line with any of the world's other highest mountains. It lies within the Sierra Maestra mountain ranges in the area of Guamá, Santiago de Cuba Province.

For those interested in hiking around Pico Turquino there are several different options available to you - but you must always have a guide! The

Sierra Maestra, which includes Pico Turquino, is still used as a military area and they don't want you to get lost and then stumble around an area you are not supposed to be in! I discovered you can hike to the summit from Santiago de Cuba, a long stretch for the more experienced, or something short and sweet like I was going to do. Outdoor hiking in Cuba is something I hope and believe will become more popular as the tourism industry booms.

And so, I booked a guided tour to hike up to the summit of Pico Turquino. I really hoped it wasn't going to be a big group – not that I minded, but it just meant I had more opportunity to ask my guide questions.

We met at the park entrance area again. Along with myself there was our guide Rolando, three French guys and a keen Australian bloke.

The day we left the wind howled and the rain poured. There were talks of the whole trip being cancelled, which made me quite disappointed because I wasn't sure if I'd get time to do the trip again.

We didn't leave till after lunch in the end, under a sky that was a thunderous grey. Rolando had forgotten his rain jacket and he didn't want to carry the heavy backpack containing all our food in the rain, so we waited for the rain to ease. I was a bit annoyed at this disorganisation. Then again, we were hiking in winter, which in Cuba is dry and reasonably cool and thus the perfect tourist season, one pleasant day after another. Unfortunately, this day wasn't dry or pleasant. In fact, it had to be the worst day, weather-wise, on my trip and even Rolando was caught out.

I was so glad that I had packed my merino top, long pants and my sleeping bag – even though the Aussie guy had laughed at me and told me I'd be fine!

Apart from all that, Rolando was a really good guide and an interesting one at that, he was the only person he told me about his personal views on the politics in Cuba.

During the four hour trek up to the hut we would be staying in Rolando and I discussed many things.

Rolando showed me a lot of the plants along the way, orchids and bromeliads. They were beautiful.

There were a lot of mosses around, which Rolando pointed out to me when it wasn't pouring, and I thought they looked just like the ones in New Zealand.

It is 18 km from the start of the hike to the top of Pico Turquino and the hut where we were to spend the night was roughly halfway. That does not sound like a great distance but but the terrain was steep, zig-zagging up and down the entire way. The rain drizzled constantly. We didn't actually see much in the way of scenery and breath-taking views because the mountain was shrouded in dismal clouds. Sometimes we would catch a brief glimpse of the peak of Pico Turquino but then it would disappear under a thick smothering of grey cloud.

The birds battled with each other and the rain to be heard and called out to each other from in the depths of trees. I kept my eyes peeled and my camera ready for them. Cuba has a lot of impressive wildlife. In terms of birds alone, there are about 350 species that frolic in the jungles and wetlands. So, it's not just for people who enjoy the challenges of hiking but for wildlife lovers too.

The Sierra Maestra Mountains held the most stunning array of birdlife I saw and heard all the way along the trail. I saw Cuban trogon, nightingale, woodpeckers, and the tiny insect-like bee hummingbirds dipping in and out of the flowers.

As the day wore on the temperature dipped and rose. The days were warm, sitting in the mid-20s (Celsius), but come nightfall the air got a bit crisp and chilly.

The tiny insect-like 'bee-hummingbirds' are an extraordinary sight

The rain began to pick up as we neared the hut and turned quickly into torrential rain, creating streams of mud running back down the path. The men in the group began to run up the track to the hut just to stay warm!

Don't underestimate the potential for cold and exposure in Cuba during the winter tourist season. The weather can change quickly and the temperatures can drop dramatically, which doesn't help if you have just got wet in an unseasonal shower of rain or 'norther'. And all this applies doubly when hiking in the mountains; where you are also likely to become damp from mist and clouds. On Pico Turquino it is not completely unknown for snow to fall; the name Turquino means 'ice mountain' in Taíno, apparently.

We were staying in a little hut called Aguada de Joaquin with bunk beds and basic amenities, at an altitude of 1,300 metres. Similar to the word 'agua', meaning water, 'aguada' in a Spanish place-name means much the same as 'waters' in English. In arid regions 'aguada' can have the significance of an oasis in the desert. But Cuba is not particularly arid, outside of a rain-shadow area on the south coast where cactus grows. The name of the hut was simply the name of a nearby mountain stream. Still, it's useful to know where you can fill up your water-bottle in the hills, and it's a good place to put a hut.

We got to the hut at about four in the afternoon and got settled in. The Australian guy who'd poked fun at me for packing all manner of warm clothing and a sleeping bag had only brought tee shirts and shorts, and he froze his butt off that night.

The front porch of the hut looked ragged and ancient, with wooden flooring that looked like it had been repaired many times over. Outside sat a lone wooden chair, the sagging seat attesting to its age.

The hut had a live-in cook and cleaner, who surprised me by wearing jandals. I asked him why he didn't have socks; I don't think he owned any socks to be honest. They had

The Aguada de Joaquin in sunshine

171

The Aguada de Joaquin camp in bad weather. The misty hillsides, sudden unhealthy chills and giant tree ferns are not only typical of higher elevations in the tropics but also, of much of New Zealand. I expected something like this, and came prepared!

their own rooms off to the side of the kitchen, there were four separate living and sleeping areas arranged in a jumble of huts. I felt sorry for them because the way it was positioned let all the wind in, and I imagined it would get really cold. They had power, at least. I have no idea where it came from, maybe solar? I asked them where the blankets where and passed them out to everyone.

The rain was so heavy. It rained all night and didn't stop until the morning. I put my things away in one of the rooms which I had all to myself. The boys set themselves up on the dining table with a pack of cards, a bottle of Havana club rum and cigars and stayed up until 11 p.m. The Aussie invited me to join in the session – as he put it, 'get written off' – so I could sleep with all the noise of the rain and wind. I politely declined and opted to continue my conversation with Rolando.

I stayed up and chatted to Rolando while we had dinner. Dinner was amazing, the food was all provided as part of the packaged tour and we had a wide selection. I was a bit wary because the kitchen did not have a fridge, and I don't think I'd eat like that again. Not because it tasted bad but I could see how it could go very wrong. I didn't get sick thank goodness – wouldn't that be an adventure further up a mountain where there were no toilets!

Rolando offered his local Cuban perspective which was made easier because he spoke English fluently; it was an interesting three-hour discussion.

He told me his father and brother lived in a poorer part of Havana. He hadn't always been a tour guide and had started out after attempting to farm land but that failed because of a drought.

His father wasn't well and that's why he started up smoking, he told me – it must have been the stress of it all. Rolando talked about his family back in Bayamo. He had two children and his wife was a social worker. He told me he smoked inside the house, that was acceptable there, and I told him he shouldn't. He agreed with me.

The first time he went up the mountain was with his father when he was 16 years old, so after all the family income issues he took up tour guiding. He made about $20 a month and supplemented his income with tips – which his family definitely need!

He told me how he had attended Fidel Castro's funeral with Communist leaders and others from all over the world. He had met a woman from France who supported Communism and told Rolando about her family ties, these being the reason why she had attended. Her family were from Spain and had been persecuted under General Franco. Like many Spanish left-wingers, they had departed for France.

I had forgotten all that history, though I knew it once. I didn't say too much to Rolando as I don't feel I know enough – well I haven't really experienced it, being from New Zealand. We talked about Justin Trudeau, the Canadian prime minister. His father, Pierre Trudeau, an earlier Prime Minister of Canada, had been good friends with the Aga Khan the Ismaili Islamic leader, they were all seen as being anti-fascist. (At Pierre Trudeau's funeral in 2000, both the Aga Khan and Fidel Castro had been honorary pall-bearers, along with former US President Jimmy Carter.) We talked about the civil war in Spain and how a lot of people were murdered.

Rolando thought that the Batista government had been fascist in its nature, similar to the Franco government in Spain. I felt a bit out of my depth with this conversation, not really knowing anything at all about Batista at the time.

We talked about the connections Cuba had with Spain and the USA, I reminded him that Cuba was very lucky to get independence, Hawaii never did!

Rolando was a very dedicated communist, for him it made complete sense. He talked about the rising middle class, something Fidel had not wanted, and he said the problem with the middle class is that they haven't learnt to share their income. He fully believed in a society where income was shared.

I talked to him about Venezuela. Rolando said a lot of Cuban doctors end up there because instead of $20 a month they get $600.

Rolando and I stayed up until about ten at night talking and eating rice biscuits, then I was driven away by the cigars and the thick smoke they created. It absolutely stunk!

I crashed out, not hearing the rain and wind howling. I did not think we would be going up to the top of the summit if the rain continued the way it was.

Talking to Rolando was far better than reading a guide book. I guess that's part of being a maverick though, you do things differently. I honestly think the best education and learning curve was by talking to taxi drivers and guides, all men, but they were open with their views and quite happy to discuss things with me.

We set out early in the morning. The sky was overcast but there was no rain. It was already beginning to warm up steadily, and the humidity hung thick in the air.

The track was littered with leaves and branches that had fallen down during the night with all the rain, and the ground was sloppy with mud.

The guys all ran the whole way up – they made it into a competition. I was quite happy taking my time and getting photos as well as continuing my conversations with Ronaldo. There were plenty of ferns, mosses and orchids at ground level which made for a beautiful scenic walk to the top.

The bush and jungle began to clear and all of a sudden, I found myself on top of Pico Turquino Mountain gazing down.

I was surprised to see a monument of José Martí, the nationally beloved Cuban revolutionist. The guys were already posing for photos there. The views were spectacular, across bushy mountains and thick jungle even if the hills were streaked by clouds.

I always refer to Cuba's forests as jungle: they are humid and thick with moisture and there are plants and trees everywhere. I found out that most of Cuba doesn't have an unrelenting dry season of the sort that would leave the landscape parched – the dryness of the winter is only relative, often punctuated by rain from fronts passing through and 'northers', and it is the cooler time of year in any case – so expect to see lots of greenery in many places, including the hike to Pico Turquino from the Bayamo side.

Having said that, the hike to Pico Turquino from the Santiago de Cuba side is more arid because it is in a rain shadow area, known in Caribbean English as 'leeward', a nautical term dating back to the days of Spanish galleons and English pirates and meaning downwind. In the Caribbean, anywhere that's 'leeward' will tend to have a dry landscape and by the same token a 'windward' locality will tend to be damp. The aridity of the Santiago de Cuba side of the range is compensated by great views of the Caribbean.

The descent was much easier, and it wasn't long before we were back in the village again. I was delighted with the trekking I had managed to get done, even amongst the howling wind and torrential rain. I stayed one more night in the hotel, $20 a night and I got breakfast and dinner included. The British couple with whom I had got the taxi ride were staying there too. We went to the restaurant and had a meal and a chat.

The woman was a doctor who had recently resigned. Her partner was a wealthy aristocrat. They couldn't decide whether to get married or not

– what they did do is drink like fish! She did have a real problem with the amount the Cuban doctors were paid, and we had some interesting discussions about the privatisation of health care in the UK.

They told me about a hotel they had stayed in that had a swimming pool and it had only cost the $18 a night! I suppose if you talk to the right people you can find some good bargains that way.

Anyway, the next morning we got into the taxi with Anley and all headed back to Bayamo, where I caught a bus to Santiago de Cuba.

CHAPTER TWELVE

Santiago de Cuba
'once rebels, now hospitable, ever heroic'

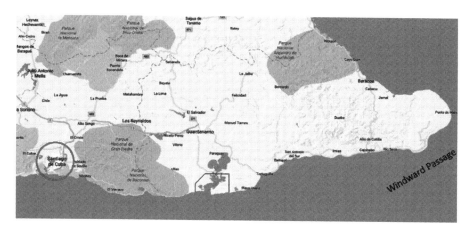

Santiago de Cuba, south-east of Bayamo and west of Guantánamo.
Map data ©2017 Google, INEGA. Words 'Windward Passage' added for this book.

S OUTH-EAST of Bayamo lies the second-largest city in Cuba, Santiago de Cuba. Santiago de Cuba is an area rich with native and African culture and I was in for another authentic Cuban experience there. The city of Santiago de Cuba has a population of roughly half a million; it is the capital of a province of the same name that has a population of a bit over a million.

Right at the start I mentioned that Santiago de Cuba was the region where much of the fighting in the 1898 Spanish-American war took place, and that the city was where the Spanish surrendered. Given that so many Cuban independence fighters also came from Santiago and its environs, most famously de Céspedes, the city now has the motto rebelde ayer, hospitalaria ahoy, heroica siempre: a phrase translated in the subtitle to this chapter.

There are plenty of package tours available now that people can do, and for some they might be better off doing it that way. For me though, I like to make my own fun and my own way around a country.

I was told you could do a hiking trip from Bayamo up through the Sierra Maestra National Park to Santiago de Cuba via Pico Turquino. That

Plaza de la Revolución, Santiago

was something I would have loved to do, but didn't because while time may have stopped in Cuba in some ways, for me, it hadn't! Instead, I organised myself to be on a bus to Santiago de Cuba, a one-and-a-half-hour bus ride from Bayamo.

The thing with Santiago de Cuba is that it is an area that is reviving and holding fast to authentic African tradition, in commemoration of all the slaves brought to Cuba by the Spanish. There is a lively Afro-Cuban culture and they have formed groups that celebrate the music, religious rites and dancing from the past. They have groups called folklórico, which have

*Graves of José Martí (top left) and Fidel Castro; monument to
Juan Almeida Bosque ("Aquí no se rinde nadie," 'here nobody
surrenders'); to the Mambisas (machete warriors); to Lt-General
Antonio Maceo y Grajales, the 'Bronze Titan' (on horseback)*

lively dancing that anyone can join in on or watch. I was looking forward to seeing all that first hand.

I arrived to a gaggle of hawkers and hustlers. It was chaos. The bus was mostly full of tourists and the hawkers were well organised around the time the buses were expected to arrive.

I got off and found myself overwhelmed by them, so I quickly pushed through the crowd until I got out onto the street a bit more. A young guy came up and said he would find me a casa to stay if I paid him $5. I thought that was pretty reasonable, so I agreed. He told me to sit down and wait and he would set out to find me one – even better. It was evening and all the streetlights were out which didn't help. I wondered how I would have gone trying to find a casa with no street lighting. I wasn't completely in the city but more on the outskirts somewhere.

The guy returned and said he found me one for $25 a night, which was brilliant. He walked me there and then happily took his $5 and headed off into the night.

The casa I stayed in was really nice and I was so grateful he had found it, although I was a bit annoyed that they didn't include breakfast in the price, which for $25 most of them do. As I was careful with where I ate, it would mean a long walk the next day trying to find somewhere that served a decent breakfast. I decided I'd head out to find myself some dinner and hopefully that meant I would find somewhere that did breakfast too.

I made my way into town with the lights all still out and found a hotel that did a delicious meal of fried chicken and salad for $3. I had decided before travelling south that I would stick to hotel-made meals because I dreaded getting sick.

Then I thought I'd go for a wander around because the lights had all come back on while I was inside eating. I headed for the famous and historical

Céspedes Park, which had been recommended to me in one of my guide books. I passed by a Cuban band on one of the streets playing some good music. Céspedes Park turned out to be a disappointment at first; it was an obscure park, square shaped and framed by taxi drivers hustling to give me a ride.

Having said that it was really a town square rather than a park, with some attractive architecture that looks best in the sun. A quiet night in which everyone had been driven indoors by failure of the street-lighting probably wasn't the best time to see it. Most of the guidebooks emphasise the social vibe. So, I left Céspedes Park and headed back to the casa for the night.

The next morning, I got up early to beat the hawkers and taxi drivers. I headed for one of the main avenues in the city, one which was famous for all its music, the Avenida General Lacret, signed as 'Gral Lacret' on the sides of buildings. Many of avenues in Santiago de Cuba are named after generals who had distinguished themselves in Cuba's thirty-year independence struggle from 1868 until 1898; more on that in a moment.

I also went and saw the beautiful port and went in search of amazing architecture. I walked past Parque Céspedes, or Céspedes Park; on the western side of the park, which is really a town square, there sat this very square white-washed chipped house. It is the oldest hacienda, or homestead, in Cuba and Latin America and was the home of the Spanish conquistador, Diego Velázquez. Built in 1516, it is now a museum.

I figured that there was so much Santiago de Cuba had to offer and a lot of it I would not get to see. It was a busy town, and there was a lot to do.

There was another major museum there as well, and more stuff about the revolution. Santiago de Cuba was known as the city of revolution, or the cradle of revolution. It was where the first slave uprising began, and played a significant role in other independence wars.

Casa Velázquez on Parque Céspedes. Top photograph by T D Lacoste, Wikimedia Commons, CC-BY-SA 3.0, taken 6 February 2005.

*The Santiago de Cuba Town Hall on Parque Céspedes, symbolic
epicentre of independence and revolution.*

Photograph by 'Chris' on Wikimedia Commons CC-BY-SA 2.0, photograph
taken on 13 May 2005. Photograph rotated one degree and slightly trimmed
for this book. Detail below from photograph above.

Santiago Cathedral on Parque Céspedes, top. Below, a view of Parque Céspedes from a hotel rooftop showing the harbour, the town hall, and Diego Velázquez's house (with shutters, at ninety degrees from the town hall), said to be the oldest Spanish structure in Latin America.

Casa Granda hotel on Parque de Céspedes and the view of the towers of the Santiago de Cuba Cathedral from the Casa Granda's roof deck.

Photograph from the roof deck by Dirk van der Made, Wikimedia Commons, CC-BY-SA 3.0, taken 23 August 2006. Architecturally rectified for this book.

*Street Music; Motorcyclists; Casa Granda, Parque Céspedes
and Santiago Cathedral by Night; and, the smaller church
of Nuestra Señora de la Caridad del Cobre*

Dry Moat of Castillo de San Pedro de la Roca; Motorcyclists.

Statue of Antonio Maceo y Grajales, with flags dipped
for the funeral of Fidel Castro

The one-storey governor's palace where the stars and stripes were run up in 1898 was replaced in 1950 by the Santiago de Cuba Town Hall. This was built in a colonial style and based on old Spanish colonial plans for a more swept-up governor's palace in Santiago. The replacement was never built under Spanish rule, no doubt because, while Santiago had been an early capital of Spanish Cuba, the seat of government had long ago shifted to Havana.

The colonial style town hall sports a balcony from which Castro first announced the success of his revolution. A couple of bronze effigies of medals now flank this balcony, reflecting Santiago's status as a hero city and the particular significance of that spot within Santiago itself.

190

Some of the Cuban generals who fought in the thirty-year struggle for independence, not only Céspedes but also such as Antonio Maceo y Grajales, came from Santiago de Cuba. General Maceo is the subject of a particularly impressive equestrian statue, set amid a rising thicket of symbolic machetes representing the Mambisas, or machete warriors who also fought for Cuba's independence.

The bay out from the city, the Bay of Santiago, was also the site of the 1898 naval battle between Spanish and US forces which eventually saw the Spanish repelled from Cuba. Decades later, on 26 June 1953 the young Fidel Castro led an armed attack on a military barracks called Moncada.

The Moncada Barracks is now a popular tourist attraction which bears the flags and portraits of Che and Castro. The next big thing to happen in the revolution was the student protests lead by a Santiago de Cuba school teacher, Frank País, in support of the overthrowing of the military dictatorship led by Batista. País was a key figure in the Castro led revolution. At the age of just 22 he was assassinated in the street by the police around a year later. The Castro government then rewarded the city for all its efforts the title of "The Heroic City".

I had seen so much all around Cuba by this stage about the revolution; flags and portraits of important figures were everywhere, on public buildings and outside people's houses. I think what surprised me with the revolution was just how passionate and generally positive the people did seem to be about it, even if they were descendants of the original Spanish rulers.

The streets around the city were quite steep and as the day wore on I got thirsty so I stopped at a bar. I sat in the back and had a non-alcoholic piña colada, with fresh coconut. I watched this amazing band with a huge cello. It was enjoyable to watch and people got up and salsa-danced to the music.

Street scene just off Céspedes park; Afro-Cuban street band.

I don't know if it has something to do with the embargo or not but there is a lot more alcohol than food in a lot of the shops and bars. There were also a lot of backpackers around who complained about paying a $2 entry fee into the restaurants and music clubs where they could enjoy live music. Obviously, this was a lot less than they would pay back home.

Santiago de Cuba's history was interesting all on its own. A lot of people had emigrated here from Haiti after the independence war between Haitians and the French, which was also the world's only successful revolt of African slaves. Haiti is only eighty-five kilometres from the eastern tip part of Cuba near Guantánamo Bay a little further to the east of Santiago, across the piratically-named Windward Passage, and on a clear night you can sometimes see the distant lights of Haiti from Cuba and vice versa. Roughly thirty thousand white Haitians moved immediately to the Santiago de Cuba area after the slaves rebelled. Afterward, many Haitians of all ethnicities came across the narrow straits and formed a distinct and persisting minority of Haitian Cubans, mostly born in Cuba but with Haitian roots. Today, three hundred thousand still Cubans speak the Haitian creole dialect of French every day, Cuba's second most widely spoken language after Spanish. Most of Haitian Cuban population lives in the eastern half of Cuba, and in the south-eastern provinces in particular.

And so, there was a really cool mix of Afro-Caribbean culture in Santiago de Cuba, in music and in the way people dressed. It was lively, busy and chaotic.

I saw many churches in Santiago de Cuba: they were everywhere! That surprised me a lot given what I had heard about Communism in general and the anti-clericalism of some past Latin revolutions. In 2017, at any rate, it seemed that Christian worshippers could practise openly and were not suppressed.

I was meant to stay another night in Santiago de Cuba, but I found it too much. I went back to my casa to organise a bus ticket and get my things. They were really good there, and asked me where I was headed.

I said I wanted to go to Guantánamo, so they put me onto another casa there for a good price, which was excellent! I got on a bus ran by Viazul and headed eastward 80kms, for one and a half hours, to the city of Guantánamo, capital of the Guántanamo province whence came the *guajira* Guantanamera, and some distance to the north of the notorious Guantánamo Bay.

CHAPTER THIRTEEN

Guantánamo

YEAH THAT BASE AND GREAT WIFI

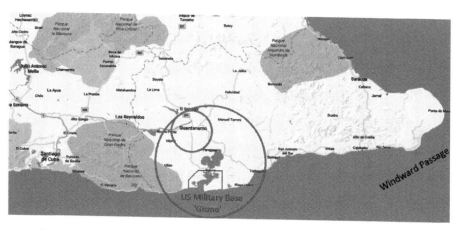

Guantánamo: the city, its environs, and the US base. Map data ©2017 Google, INEGA. Words entirely on blue background added for this book.

THE bus ride to the city of Guantánamo was short and sweet, and I wasn't really sure what I to expect there.

The Guantánamo province has two major cities of Guantánamo and Baracoa, and occupies a bit over six thousand square kilometres. The total population of the Guantánamo province is around half a million, or about the same as the city of Santiago de Cuba.

I got to the bus station and it was relatively quiet. There was nothing around really, not compared to the other places. There were a few tiny road side stalls where you could buy coconut crackers and a glass of yogurt, and it was a good ten-minute walk to the taxi stand.

There was a guy on his motorbike, the first I'd seen, and he offered to get me to my casa for $3. I agreed and hopped on.

I went straight to my casa and booked in; thankfully my room was not taken. It cost me $25 a night, had a fridge, and was one of the nicer casas I had stayed in! The couple who ran it offered to chaperone me around. I said, no I'll go on my own. I figured they had friends down the road, who they could profit from for taking me there.

I didn't want to be hassled into going somewhere I didn't want to so I set out on my own, even though the wife and her daughter followed me down the road for a little while.

Walking around I thought Guantánamo was underrated, there were no tourists around – which was great and the more I saw the more I liked it.

Guantánamo was beautiful I must say. The area was founded in 1791 and in Taíno it translates to land between rivers. It was an interesting city with a lot of construction going on when I passed through.

There was a big highway being built to connect Guantánamo more directly with Havana, in the hope that it would encourage more tourists to visit there.

The buildings were not quite like the other cities. Many people liken it to the French Quarter in Louisiana, and I could see the resemblance.

There were not many English-speaking people there, but that was fine. I still managed find my way around. I really wanted to see Guantánamo Bay, the US military base that has been used to house detainees since the beginning of the so called 'War on Terror'. There is a lot of debate surrounding the base and everyone has their opinions on it.

I did not plan to visit the American base, but I had heard that it was possible to get a good view of it from a Cuban lookout on a ridge, so I decided to go there.

I chanced upon this guy who was dressed like a Jamaican and walked around with that Rasta swag, only to find out he was just a local. I told him I wanted to have a look at the American Guantánamo base so he walked around with me helping me find transport.

I found the problem was finding a taxi to take me to the lookout. Many of them wouldn't because of the drive. It was quite a mission to get there, apparently. I soon saw that for myself.

I found a driver in the end, thanks to my Jamaican-Cuban friend; he was a local with a bright red classic car, a 1980s model. It was a one hour ride up a windy road up a mountain.

He told me the issue is if you're a taxi driver then you get charged a fee for passing through a Cuban military checkpoint, although if you travel on a bus with a tour company they don't charge them. As for private travellers, they quite often get turned back.

I paid the driver $10 and off we went. The road was quite steep and wove up around a big hill. We were duly intercepted by the Cuban military, and the driver told them I was his wife and he was taking me for a drive. That surprisingly worked and we were allowed to continue on our way. Eventually we came to a small restaurant set up for tour buses and a viewing tower from which the American base could be viewed. Apparently, you could also get a good view from a hotel nearby that was set up just for that. There was a local guy there who agreed to show me around on the Cuban side. He was taking his cousin to look at the base as well, and luckily for me he spoke fluent English.

He talked to me about what he knew of Fidel Castro's family. I had no idea Castro had so many children to so many different women. He was very private about his family life until they were all old enough to talk about it to the media.

197

Guantánamo regional sign, and street scene.

Photograph of sign is from Pixabay, CC0 public domain. Photograph of street scene ('Hotel Washington') by Leon Petrosyan, Wikimedia Commons, CC-BY-SA 3.0, photograph apparently taken 18 June 2004.

Guantánamo residential areas, with casa particular at top.

Piviso images CC0 public domain, 2015 top, 2017 bottom. Top image slightly architecturally rectified and cropped for this book.

The local guy told me his worry was that after Raúl Castro stepped down that his son would become the next President of Cuba, and he wasn't sure what kind of leader he would be. I think that was everyone's worry: who would be the next Cuban President and what would change. He said a lot more of the younger generations were getting involved again and becoming interested in left-wing ideals. In his view, the Castro regime was fine at managing provinces but when it came to an entire country, that's where it ran into issues.

He walked with me to the tower that overlooks the base, and I came across a display of photos that had been smuggled out of the Guantánamo prison by Cuban workers. So, I spent a bit of time wandering about and looking at them. Some were quite haunting, and I took some photos of those.

Guantánamo Bay: A Closer View.

Imagery ©2017 CNES/Astrium, Cnes/SpotImage, DigitalGlobe,
Landsat/Copernicus, U.S. Geological Survey. Map data ©2017 Google

How the American base at Guántanamo came about is an interesting story. As I mentioned earlier, after the war of independence, which ended in 1898 with American intervention, the Cubans found themselves living in a *de facto* protectorate of the United States. The Cuban legislature of that

Cuban observation tower, overlooking the American base at Guantánamo ('Gitmo'), at top. Smuggled photograph of 'Gitmo' detainee, displayed near the tower, at bottom.

era ceded the Guantánamo base to the USA in 1903 on a perpetual lease that can only be voided by mutual agreement. The lease costs the USA a peppercorn sum of few thousand dollars a year and since 1960, the Castro administration has not cashed the annual cheques in any case.

The Americans first noticed the qualities of Guantanamo Bay, perhaps, when the American fleet involved in the Spanish-American war took shelter there during the 1898 hurricane season. A *Time* magazine article of 28 March 1960 describes Guantanamo Bay as the US Navy's "best natural harbour south of Charleston, S.C." American personnel nick-name the area Gitmo.

In 2002, US President George W. Bush established a prison, or detention camp, on the base for detainees captured during the so-called 'War on Terror'.

President Obama wanted to close the facility; his administration did manage to bring the number of detainees down from 245 to 41. Now, President Trump wants to expand the prison.

There has been more debate about the prison's status in the wake of the 2017 elections in the USA. International human rights groups have recommended that the US shut down the base and leave. I have heard it is like a miniature US city, with its own food being imported, and that at one point they had to import water too. The Cubans shut off the water supply to the base to try to get them to leave.

A flamboyant, left-wing American journalist named Michael Moore tried to enter the base once: they wouldn't let him in. He then went on to make a documentary in 2007 called Sicko which compared the US standards of health care to other countries, including Cuba's. It involved a few scenes of him attempting to enter the Guantánamo base, without luck. I think that helped shed light on the secrecy surrounding the place at the time.

The boundary between Castroite Cuba and the American base is one of the last remaining militarised Cold War frontiers, a bit like North versus South Korea or the former Berlin Wall. All the same, I was told that the troops of both sides get together once a month over beers to discuss whether there have been any issues that might cause trouble. I doubt that happens in Korea, or for that matter that it was common in Europe in the old days either.

(A bit later on I had an eye-opening experience that made me realise how small the world is, or the world of 'army brats' in any case. I was at the Hawai'i international airport, which is where I headed straight after Cuba. I had some of the photos I'd taken at the museum at Guantanamo Bay and I showed the pictures to a couple of people at the airport with whom I'd struck up a conversation. One of them pointed to a man in one photo and said, that is my step-father! That was so amazing, weird and funny at the same time. Life is full of surprises.)

When I was in Guantánamo, the guy who went on the tour with me and his cousin told me about the best places to visit locally. He'd been fantastic, so I shouted them a beer at the restaurant before heading back into Guantánamo town.

Out wandering as I do I found the Plaza de la Revolución. There were many privately-run restaurants in Guantánamo town, although the grocery stores were still ran by the government. I noticed they sold a lot more alcohol then they did food in them too.

Nirvana! I found Wifi seemed to be more available here than anywhere else I had been. There were a whole lot of guys selling Wi-Fi off their computers, small businesses making money. I spent four hours online doing work stuff.

I went around some of the bakeries and was disappointed with the produce because it was all coated in sugar, so I didn't eat anything from there.

I went into one shop and was approached by a beggar, I was quite taken aback and I didn't know what to do. It was the first one I had seen in all of Cuba.

Back at my casa I was in my room when there was a knocking at the door. I peered around the door to see the owner opening up and buying some ice cream from a lady standing on the doorstep. She offered me some and although I was hesitant about what I was eating, it was hot and I felt like it!

So, we sat down and had ice cream together. It was delicious even though I thought if I'm going to have tummy troubles this will do it to me! A few seconds later another lady knocked on the door, this time selling bread. I haven't experienced this before, but it just added to the old-fashioned charm of the area. The further south you go, the more the clocks get wound back. It was refreshing.

I found another government hotel in Guantánamo town and ate there for only $3; it was another delicious meal of fried chicken. I sat back and enjoyed the live music and to my delight the band played traditional Cuban music.

I ordered one more beer at one of the hotels before I left. I was headed to Baracoa, east of Guantánamo. Apparently, the beaches there were the best in all of Cuba. In view of the standard set by dozens of other Cuban seaside resorts from Varadero to the equally crystalline Playa Daiquiri (I must make a point of watching the sun go down there!), to say that Baracoa had the best beaches in Cuba was surely a large claim to make.

The other reason I wanted to go to Baracoa was because it was home to the only remaining indigenous community in Cuba. I had heard some pretty intense stories about how most of the indigenous people had died out because of European diseases and oppression in the 1500s and beyond. The few who remained had mostly intermarried into the now-dominant Spanish-speaking populations and lost their language and identity, in fact to the point that the Taíno language is forgotten apart from the various words it has contributed to the vocabulary of other languages – hurricane, barbecue, hammock, and so on – and this was the pattern throughout the Caribbean.

Everything indigenous in Cuba today is thus, strictly speaking, a sort of cultural revival even if most of the population are in fact at least partly Taíno by descent, and a revival devoid of the key ingredient, the language. The Spanish colonisers never bothered to systematically record it, in contrast to the nineteenth-century missionaries who made the most careful study of the Māori language in New Zealand, for example, and thus contributed greatly to its survival. Of course, that was in a later, more scientific era as well as a somewhat more humane one.

I thought after Baracoa I would like to fly back to Havana if I could. They had a small airport there that made national flights. My taxi driver warned me that the flights from the smaller towns could be quite dodgy and that while the locals knew all about the missing planes, they weren't so open with the tourists about it. I thought I'd still give it a crack though, as I was over long bus rides, and Baracoa to Havana would be what I imagined to be a horrific twenty-hour bus ride.

CHAPTER FOURTEEN

Baracoa

'THE MOST BEAUTIFUL LAND'

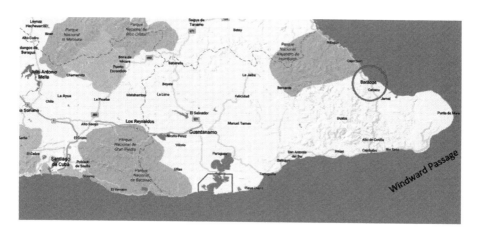

Baracoa, east of Guantánamo. Map data ©2017 Google, INEGA.
Words 'Windward Passage' added for this book.

AMAZEMENT is what followed when I arrived in Baracoa. I had been told the next stop on my list was a city in ruins. Why? Because Hurricane Matthew had gone through the region in October 2016, and the city and people were still recovering. Well, when I arrived, it was not a city in ruins at all. Yes, there were some areas of debris and flattened palm trees and the stadium was still in disrepair. But for the most part it was beautiful! Baracoa is a generally beautiful area not far from Guantánamo: two hours on the bus was all it took.

Images of Hurricane Matthew devastation in Baracoa, October 2016.
Courtesy Cuba4, a Catholic aid agency.

The Road to Baracoa (La Farola), opened in 1965.

Photograph by Lagaly de (Sigi Knoll), Wikimedia
Commons, CC-BY-SA 3.0, taken 31 March 2008

Out on a limb from Guantánamo, Baracoa sits looking out across the
Atlantic Ocean. It was tropical like the rest of Cuba, but there was definitely
something different about the place, a combination of its isolation from the
rest of Cuba (it was only connected to the national road network as late
as 1965), verdant lushness (this is the wettest part of Cuba), and an Afro-
Caribbean culture influenced by proximity to Haiti.

It was the first city founded in Cuba by the conquistador Velázquez in
1511, and also supposedly the first place where Columbus first set foot on
Cuba in 1492, although a certain amount of vagueness is attached to the
precise spots where Columbus made his early landfalls.

Columbus was, of course, the most famously lost of the all major
explorers. He thought he had arrived somewhere in the vicinity of China,
and in 1492 had not had a chance to map any neighbouring lands to get his

209

bearings, even in a local sense. Many of his detailed logbook records were misplaced or destroyed, and the navigational instruments of the day were useless for determining a ship's east-west position on the globe, although they enabled people to tell how far north or south they were and, for that matter, what direction was north.

Wherever it was that he stepped ashore precisely, Columbus declared that "this is the most beautiful land that human eyes have ever seen," praising a site with a good port, abundant fresh water and plentiful wood, overlooked by a flat-topped mountain. Ever since, the honour of being the most beautiful land that human eyes have ever seen has been disputed between Baracoa and the province of Holguín immediately to its north. Most scholars, apparently, side with Baracoa, because a flat-topped mountain is a perfect description of the one the Spanish later named El Yunque, the Anvil, which prominently overlooks Baracoa.

'The Most Beautiful Land': Baracoa and El Yunque (the Anvil), the prominent local table mountain.

Cropped Pivisio image, CC0 public domain, taken 8 December 2015.

Taíno monument at the Paradise Caves

Baracoa was still recovering from Hurricane Matthew when I was there.

The trees on the hills in the background are largely stripped of leaves in this photograph, and therefore don't look as green as they should (January 2017)

Not all the backstreets of Baracoa
are paved as yet.

There are only a bit over 80,000 permanent residents in Baracoa, so it is a relatively small city. Nice enough though, that I felt like I had found one of Cuba's best kept secrets. Indeed, until 1965 Baracoa enjoyed no road connection with the rest of Cuba; it is still something of a hide-away.

I ended up staying in a government hotel, this time.

Giant Tree Ferns on El Yunque.

Photograph by Dirk van der Made (DirkvdM) on Wikimedia Commons,
CC-BY-SA 3.0 Photograph probably taken 7 August 2006.

There was a lot of native culture in the area, well preserved from many historical sites. The indigenous group, the Taíno people, still live in the area, and I was told they keep to themselves – not to be anti-social but to preserve their culture and identity. They put on shows and performances for the tourists that do come to Baracoa.

I noticed there were many chocolate cafes selling chocolate drinks. I was envious as I watched people sipping them contentedly. I don't do dairy, and I got a bit fed up because all I wanted was a coffee and I couldn't find any!

In Cuba, they have lines for everything, and this especially noticeable in Baracoa! You have to wait in a line to just buy bread, even at the bakeries, which are filled again with sugary food. In fact, I met a German lady who had brought all her own food with her because she was gluten intolerant – like me.

I became unwell shortly after arriving in Baracoa and I couldn't seem to shake it. I don't know if it was the fruit juice or that ice cream in Guantánamo or if it was the flounder I had eaten the first night at my hotel. Whatever did it, it got me good and proper.

Even though I wasn't feeling overly well and had dosed up on anti-diarrhoea pills I still got out to see the indigenous area that I had wanted to see. It turned out to be a cave on a hill, which was used as a grave site for slaves, part of a museum. I don't really know what my thoughts were on that, I was quite lost for words. It was the darker side of Cuban history that was quite overwhelming. The museum was interesting. It showed a lot of the indigenous history of the Taíno Indian peoples. It was in some caves and its English-language name was 'The Paradise Cave Museum of the Indigenous People'.

It was a really memorable experience, the earthy smells as you look at ancient artefacts, the coolness of the cave walls around you, the dim lighting

– it made for a different experience. It showed Taíno skeletons in glass cases (I think they may have been replicas) pottery and art work. I thought it was quite cool because everything was in caves hidden away in the bush. There were sculptures of the people washing clothes and of what I what I assumed were their gods. From the entrance if you looked out past the bush and tall trees, you got a birds-eye view across Baracoa and the Atlantic Ocean in the distance, a blue-grey unlike the turquoise water in Havana.

Slavery wasn't abolished in Cuba until 1886, with slaves brought by the colonist from Africa to work on the booming sugar cane industries. Over a million African people were brought to Cuba during this time as part of the Atlantic Slave Trade. During the Spanish reign over Cuba, they put out laws about work hours, food provisions, and clothing and forbade the sale of young children that gave the slaves some better quality of life. I wonder whether anyone in Cuba actually obeyed those laws, because the history of slavery in Cuba is marked by a lot of uprisings.

There is a lot for the traveller to enjoy around Baracoa: national parks, stunning mountain ranges and river tours. I would have definitely done more, had I been feeling better.

There are four main rivers that cut through the land surrounding Baracoa. You can do heaps of boat tours, swimming and other water activities in the Rivers Yumuri, Miel, Macaguanigua, and Duaba, which are usually pristine and clear, fed by the lush rain forest and running straight down to the sea.

I went for a swim in one of the rivers there; I need to cool off in all the heat and humidity. It was lovely and just what I needed. I travelled down the coast a bit on a local bus and went and saw a cocoa plantation – that explained all the chocolate cafes around the town.

I saw firsthand evidence of the African Vodou or Santería religion in Baracoa. There were small shrines with dolls and shells arranged artfully

Top Image: Baracoa and environs with wide, white banks of the Rivers Toa (northernmost) and Duaba (in middle) clearly visible, plus El Yunque, casting dark shadow, at bottom left. Bottom Image: Baracoa and bay to east with interesting landform of marine terraces to right, typical of Cuban coasts near the Windward Passage and indicating strong uplift. Each dark line in terraces is a cliff, in shadow, overlooking an ancient beach and coastal shallows now literally high and dry.

Source: Google Earth. Imagery ©2017 CNES/Astrium, TerraMetrics (+ Data SIO, NOAA, U.S. Navy, NGA, GEBCO, top image only). Map data ©2017 Google.

*A shrine to the Sea Queen, a dead tree on the
shoreline, and street art in Baracoa.*

which was really interesting! I saw one that I snapped a quick photo of, a local explained to me this was the 'Sea Queen'.

I saw a few just on the side of the road or by the beach; it was interesting but a bit freaky at the same time. The Haitians who were originally from Africa brought with them the practice and when they immigrated to Cuba it became popular there too. This was particularly true in the southern areas of Cuba, which are the closest to Haiti.

Another important piece of local religious symbolism is the Cruz de Parra, the 'vine cross', the only one of the 29 crosses left around the island by Christopher Columbus. It is so called because Diego Velázquez's men found it covered in vines a couple of decades after Columbus had left it in Baracoa. It probably wasn't easy to miss, as it was originally two metres high. The

218

Baracoa Cathedral before and after restoration / Cruz de Parra.

Top and middle images photographed by Jorge E. San Roman. As 'Baracoa Cathedral Square' and 'Cruz de la Parra', Wikimedia Commons, CC-BY-SA 2.5, pictures taken on or before 11 May 2006. Top image architecturally rectified and slightly cropped for this book. Bottom image is Piviso CC0 public domain

A painting of Columbus on his flagship of discovery the Santa Maria, the largest of three vessels, that suggests why there wasn't room to lug dozens of large crosses over from Spain (or inded, much room for anything else)

Emmanuel Leutze, 'Christopher Columbus on Santa Maria in 1492' (1855), public domain Wikimedia image

surviving Cruz de Parra is far stubbier, because bits were continually whittled away by souvenir hunters and those in search of good luck charms – the probable fate of the other crosses as well – until the ends of the arms were eventually capped with silver and the cross installed in the local cathedral, a small building which has lately been renovated like much else in Cuba.

To guard against the possibility of venerating a fake, the Cruz de Parra has been carbon-dated and found to be of the right period, in the sense that the latest possible date of the harvest of the wood was 1530 and the most likely date somewhat earlier, although it is made of local wood. If the cross had been of great antiquity and made of Spanish oak that would have been the clincher. But then again, it's inconceivable that Columbus would have carried 29 bulky crosses all the way over from Spain in his surprisingly small ships. A replica of the Cruz de Parra, in its stubby form, can also be seen at an outdoor location in Baracoa.

Many among Columbus's crews were Galicians, from the north-western Atlantic province of Spain known in English as Galicia, where the city of Santiago de Compostela is located, a province less arid than other parts of Spain, where there was also an abundance of wood for making ships, and important ports like Vigo and A (La) Coruña. Santiago means 'Saint James' in the Galician language, which is similar to Portuguese, as does San Diego in the Castilian form of Spanish historically spoken by landlubbers in the interior regions of Spain, such as the inhabitants of Madrid. Columbus's flagship the Santa Maria was built in Galicia and originally named the Gallego, the Galician.

There is a strong Galician influence on Latin America to this day, with several times more Santiagos than San Diegos on the map of the Americas, even if one of the San Diegos is itself a famous naval port. Even Fidel and Raúl Castro's father Angel was a Galician who emigrated to Cuba as a young man after serving there in the Spanish army, whether this is a coincidence or not. The nautical, Galician connection with the New World has something in common with the fact that many English-speaking Americans originally came from the more western, Atlantic and seafaring parts of the British Isles; from Plymouth to Plymouth Rock as we might say.

Like Captain Cook's much later Endeavour, the Santa Maria was a second-hand coastal trader not actually designed to sail the ocean blue. One gets the feeling that both expeditions were done on the cheap, their eventual importance greatly underestimated to begin with. When we think that Caribbean hurricanes were un-heard of in Europe, obviously, in Columbus's time, his crews were fortunate not to have been lost at sea.

As if to set an unfortunate precedent, Columbus, who made four voyages to the 'Indies' as he imagined them to be, was guilty of many cruelties toward the 'Indians' of the island of Quisqueya or Hispaniola, the first island to be colonised in earnest by the Spanish. When word of this filtered back home he was thrown in jail and stripped of the title of governor of the territories he had claimed for Spain.

A bust of Hatuey by the Cuban sculptor Rita Longa, unveiled in Baracoa's Independence Park in 1953.

Both images from Wikimedia Commons, CC-BY-SA 2.5. The photograph on the left was taken by Tommy Huynh on 29 May 2006. The photograph on the right was taken by Michał Zalewski on 17 September 2005.

For all his achievements, Columbus died in disgrace and obscurity in 1506. Mistreatment of the locals was not yet something to which the newly founded Spanish empire would turn a blind eye. That is, not yet. As with the United States, so it seems that many abuses were not inherent to Spain as such but really grew hand in hand with the cultivation of an empire, along the lines of the saying that 'power corrupts, and absolute power corrupts absolutely'.

In 1511 a Taíno cacquique, or chief, named Hatuey came across the Windward Passage from Quisqueya to warn the Cuban Taíno about their likely fate at the hands of the Spanish. Hatuey was followed shortly thereafter by Velázquez, who unwitting founded the settlement of Baracoa in the very same region where Hatuey had preached his message of resistance some weeks or months before. The Taíno, led by Hatuey, besieged the infant Spanish settlement from the instant of its foundation, and so Hatuey was in that sense the first rebel in the Americas and the first Cuban national hero (even if he was from what is now Haiti or the Dominican Republic).

Captured by Velázquez, Hatuey was burned alive at the stake at a place called Yara. Most say that this happened in a Yara near Bayamo, about 250 km west of Baracoa; but I notice that a plaque on the statue of Hatuey in Baracoa says that he was "immolado in Yara de Baracoa," a place much closer to Baracoa. Each location has its champions in this tug-of-war and both Yara (near Bayamo) and Baracoa have their own statue of Hatuey, each very good. The story told from the 1500s onward by the Spanish themselves was that to a priest trying to convert him to Christianity right at the end, Hatuey said he would rather go to Hell than to Heaven, if Heaven was full of Spaniards.

Towards the end of my stay in Baracoa I went to stay in a casa. We had the same people knocking at the doors and selling their wares, eggs, tomatoes and watermelons. I brought some but I did not eat the watermelon.

The lady running it said it was a blessing when her husband died because he used to sleep around and broke her heart – she even told me that in front of her sons – I didn't know what to say to that!

This is another aspect of Cuban machismo. I've heard it's not normal but still accepted for men to have two wives and the older one stays at home minding the kids. Apparently. there are a lot of sixteen-year-old single mothers in Cuba. A lot of men knock them up and then shoot through, which is quite sad really. And then of course there was the strange campaign of persecution of homosexuals that went on for a while under the Castro regime, rather odd for a regime that was otherwise backed by every political progressive from Stockholm to San Francisco (though Fidel later on confessed that it had been wrong).

All in all, much in Cuban society really did seem to revolve around the concept of being a real man, defined in essence as a sort of bandit or pirate, a 'pistolero' who stands up to the rich and powerful whether we are speaking of Spanish grandees or re-colonising Americans as the adversary, and a ladies' man as well.

The casa proprietor was a nice enough lady in spite of a degree of bitterness about her late husband's shortcomings. She told me how her son was a tattoo artist in town. She wanted to help support him by building that business up too.

She also warned me that there were a lot of men walking around in their sixties and older with a beautiful twenty-year-old on their arms, and that it wasn't unusual to see that. Many western men turn up there and I ran into a couple of them in a restaurant one night.

It was a disgusting conversation, I overheard them talking to each other discussing woman in a really off-putting fashion. They were both from Canada and in their seventies and were talking about these younger women and it was just beyond creepy, I turned around and I said to them; well I hope you don't even think about touching those young girls. They went on to tell me they had given these young girls $15,000 to start up their own casas and then the two Canadian men would come and go as they pleased.

The ambiguities of a piratical definition of manhood among Cuban men was one thing. But it goes without saying that this kind of sex tourism came with a whole new level of added yuck factor.

In town, I tried to access the Wifi again to make calls but there were huge lines at the store that sold the cards and you were only allocated 30 minutes per person.

I met at lady who had been doing tours to Baracoa from the US for about 15 years which I thought was quite interesting. She would organise all these group tour packages, and she must have sorted something out with their visas because I would have thought that would have been a problem for Americans.

I went to the bus stop as my time was nearing an end in Cuba and I needed to make a start on heading back towards Havana. I thought I would break the trip up by stopping in Camagüey on the way back.

Take note: get used to hot, uncomfortable, dusty, and very long bus rides when in Cuba!

CHAPTER FIFTEEN

Camagüey

LOVELY ART TOWN, ON MY LIST TO GO BACK

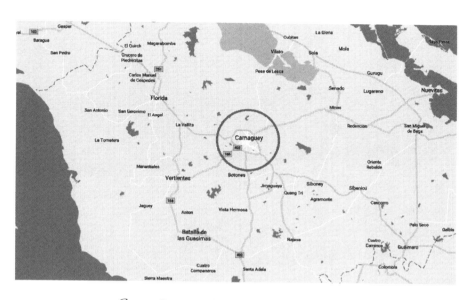

Camagüey. Map data ©2017 Google, INEGA

I T was a seven-hour bus ride from Baracoa to Camagüey. That was all
it took, but it felt much longer because I was not feeling the greatest.

Camagüey was a beautiful surprise: a rustic colonial-era town where art
flourished. It was an area I found, where the revolution was not flagged as
prominently as in other areas I had visited.

There was a Southern-USA feel to Camagüey, especially in the more
rural areas where cattle ranches popped up in place of the usual sugarcane
and tobacco plantations.

The area around Camagüey was completely flat, much to my surprise. Actually, this is typical of a lot of Cuba. But most of the towns and cities I had spent time in had very noticeable hills around them up to this point. Cows were grazing contently on the green grass, under a Caribbean sun.

In the 1700s the Spanish had a plan to dig a ship canal across the middle of Cuba to the west of Camagüey. The sea journey from Havana to Cienfuegos would have been dramatically shortened, and Cuba no doubt converted into an absolutely impregnable stronghold of the Spanish Americas, ships hiding in the canal and capable of exit either to the north or to the south. However, the plan was too ambitious for the time, and by the time it became practical, the railways had begun to offer an alternative. Batista revived the idea in the 1950s, but it was seriously anachronistic by then, offering only a modest saving on sea routes that otherwise used the Windward Passage.

'The Towne of Puerto del Principe taken & Sackt', by Henry Morgan in 1668.

I am not sure how accurate this widely reproduced image is, as it is hard to think of any large hills near Camagüey. This image appears in John Masefield, *On the Spanish Main*, London & Edinburgh, 1906, via the English Wikipedia entry on Camagüey.

228

La Iglesia de Nuestra Señora de la Soledad, before and after restoration.
Top Image: Photograph by Danleo, Wikimedia Commons, CC-BY-2.5,
taken on or before 1 March 2006. Architecturally rectified and cropped
as necessary for rectification. Bottom Image: Photograph by Tango 7174,
Wikimedia Commons CC-BY-4.0, taken on 9 January 2007

229

I was surprised by all the churches here, mostly Catholic, which added to the charm of Camagüey. The old part of the city seems maze-like and devoid of any overall street plan, and one explanation for the maze of streets is that they were laid out purely in reference to the nearest church and without much thought as to how people might get across town.

Another explanation is that this was done to confuse invading pirates. Oddly enough, although the city is 80 km inland, it was known throughout the Spanish colonial era as Puerto [del] Principe or 'Prince's Port', and it was even attacked by Captain Morgan in 1668. For in fact the town had been founded on the north coast, and moved inland after pirate attacks. Captain Morgan followed it inland!

All the same, the idea that the confusing layout of this inland city was designed to frustrate pirate attacks sounds 'a likely story' to me, and I favour the lack-of-planning theory: that it probably just grew out of a collection of small parish communities that conglomerated together. It seems as though Spanish government authority and settlement in the early days was very much concentrated on the two ends of the island, the Havana end and the Santiago end, where there were good ports, and that the centre of the island was a sort of 'Wild West'.

That would have been another reason for a canal, which looks as though it would probably have gone through in the vicinity of the cities of Ciego de Ávila (founded in 1840) and Morón, a line that would become a major Spanish defensive line during the nineteenth century wars of liberation, a line of forts known as the 'Trocha', or cutoff.

The remoteness of central Cuba in earlier times may also explain why town planning in strict accordance with La Traza, the orderly Spanish colonial town planning system, wasn't applied to Camagüey.

Like other cities in Cuba, Camagüey has produced many a person worthy of national pride. The local list includes Ignacio Agramonte, a hero of the early independence wars who fell in battle in 1873, the subject of a spectacular equestrian statue best seen from the front, and Ana Betancourt, an early feminist and independence supporter exiled to Spain in 1871 who never saw her homeland again. Another was Carlos J. Findlay, a local doctor who at the beginning of the 1880s developed the idea that yellow fever – a fatal disease of the damper parts of tropical America – was spread by mosquitos. Findlay even correctly identified the sort of mosquito that was the chief culprit in spreading the disease.

Findlay had difficulty *proving* his theory, however, with the result that Cuba's Spanish rulers took little notice. It was not until the Spanish-American war of 1898, one fortunate outcome of which was that it brought some American experts on yellow fever to Cuba, including the famous Walter Reed, that the dread disease would be tamed.

The Americans picked up on Findlay's theory at last. Under the Americans, mosquito eradication began in earnest in Havana in 1901, with a drop in the death rate noticeable by 1902. At the same time, Findlay was proven to be right, not only by such results but by other scientific means that the Americans had at their disposal.

While all that might be seen as evidence of the energetic character of the new American administration compared to the indolence of the previous Spanish one (which is certainly how American politicians anxious to justify the war represented such changes), and while most Americans would later believe Reed to be the conqueror of yellow fever, in fact both Reed and the American military governor of Cuba were fulsome in their praise of Findlay, who had already solved about three quarters of the problem before they stepped ashore and pointed them in the right direction straight away. In this sense, Findlay was more highly honoured than the unfortunate general García, the one who was snubbed at Santiago de Cuba.

Pedestrianised streets (top) and Plaza de los Trabajadores (bottom).

Bottom Image: Arnoud Joris Maaswinkel, on Wikimedia Commons, CC-BY-SA 4.0. Architecturally rectified and slightly cropped.

Camagüey Street Art, including images of Ana Betancourt, Carlos J Findlay (with glasses) and Ignacio Agramonte (with moustache).

Top Image: Yulka-Lucia, Wikimedia Commons, CC-BY-SA 4.0, taken 29 March 2013. Cropped top and bottom.

233

The Panama Canal, impossible to build hitherto because the workers would have perished from yellow fever, now became a possibility as well.

Camagüey is also the home of an internationally acclaimed ballet company, housed in the splendid Teatro Principal.

The city was a place that appeared on first sights to fully embrace the modernisation that was becoming more and more apparent all over Cuba. Once a backwater, it was now a bustling centre with a rising population of more than three hundred thousand.

Camagüey has recently made it to the UNESCO World Heritage list in 2014, another historical gem in Cuba, because of its well-preserved city centre.

I got off the bus and found a casa, then headed out to explore. I needed a brief stop before another twelve-hour bus ride from Camagüey to Havana. I needed to shave my legs so I went out looking for a razor, I found some in one of the government-run stores and the cheapest was $30! I thought flag that, and just left it until Hawaii.

So, I don't know if it is just Camagüey but some things were incredibly expensive, especially through the government-run stores.

What I found with Camagüey though, apart from it being slightly on the expensive side, is that it had some of the best museums in Cuba.

There are two main art gallery museums, the Museo de la Cerámica Artística Contemporánea and the Galería Taller Martha Jiménez Pérez. Both sit in the heart of the city centre and are easily in walking distance from one another.

Although Camagüey was another city founded by the famed Spanish conqueror, Diego Velázquez in 1524 (as Puerto Principe), the relocated town eventually regained the original Taíno name of the locality as Cuba became independent, in 1903. Camagüey is a Taíno word meaning 'descended from the Camagua', a tree sacred to the Taíno; it also reflects the name of a chief named Camagüeybax who had been hospitable to the first Spanish settlers in what is now the Camagüey region. I suppose that when you have a country that is colonised, some of the original names of places or their meanings get lost - so it was good to see that this was still remembered and commemorated.

In fact, there is such a rich history to the area surrounding Camagüey, that it would spark interest for any student.

At one time the locals possessed large numbers of clay bottles called tinajónes, which they used to collect rain water. The lack of mountains nearby must mean that local streams are feeble and prone to drying up. Nowadays the tinajónes have become part of the culture, and are used in decoration and art works. A local saying holds that anyone who drinks water from a tinajón will fall in love with a local person and never leave. (Actually, in Baracoa they have a similar legend concerning the water from their clear rivers.)

(Tinajón looks a lot like the English word 'demijohn' meaning a large bottle; maybe that's where demijohn comes from.)

Thus Camagüey is known as the city of 'alleys and tinajónes'

Camagüey has surprising Catholic connections, beginning with the visit of Pope John Paul II in 1998. It was also the host city for the celebration of Cuba's first saint, Fray José Olallo, in 2008.

What I did notice about Camagüey is that there was a lot of renovation going on, and that was really nice to see. The people seemed to really love their city, their buildings and architecture.

I did not get out as much as I would have liked to in Camagüey. Due to food poisoning, I was mostly focused on getting some rest before the twelve-hour bus journey back to Havana.

Camagüey Tinajónes, in front of the city sign and as a souvenir.

Top Image: Pixabay, CC0 public domain. Bottom Image: Arnoud Joris Maaswinkel, Wikimedia Commons, CC-BY-SA 4.0, taken 5 April 2015

CHAPTER SIXTEEN
Conclusion

W HEN the time came to depart, I had mixed feelings about leaving Cuba. I had well and truly been surprised by the country, and all my previous presumptions had been blown out the water.

It is a country still trying to catch up with modern technology and the Internet, a mixture of old and modern. And I got the feeling that many Cubans are quite happy living in a Communist-run society, perhaps because those who aren't have already left.

While it does take a while to get your head around Cuban realities, I was glad I put aside my prejudgements.

Talking with taxi drivers and local people was the best thing I did. I got an understanding from all the different people I encountered there, and that was truly a good lesson. It was good to get people talking. I learned that the government gives a lot of Cubans food rations so even the poorest people are still healthy and well fed!

The government now allows people to run their own private businesses such as taxi services and the *casas particulares*, and I even met a woman who owned a part of the only chocolate factory in Cuba. I don't know what part of it she actually owns, whether it was the farm or the right to conduct tours, but it was interesting.

Another reason for happiness, surely, is that most of the people live in convivial cities and towns built on an ancient pattern, cities and towns not yet rendered hostile by sprawling suburbs and huge numbers of automobiles. There do not yet seem to be any traffic jams in Cuba. To borrow one of Mark Twain's expressions, those are the 'modern inconveniences' that have isolated people from each other and shredded nerves in many a large city in the West, including my native Auckland – but not yet in Cuba.

Not *yet.* . It will be a challenge for Cuba to develop economically, as it surely needs to, and yet preserve its current sociable and charming character. Cuba's future leaders should keep a copy of the old Joni Mitchell song about having 'paved paradise and put up a parking lot' on hand, and play it often. Perhaps they will be able to avoid the mistakes made in other countries, not least because the government is strong and supports planning.

Cuba, a country where most people are still leading eighteenth-century lives in many respects, is a place where it is as if we might yet rewind the tape of becoming modern, and start over with more knowledge of what to do and what not to do. Conquering diseases and illiteracy, yes. Ruining the city with cars and motorways and sprawling suburbs, no.

Finally, one unfortunate thing that I did find very noticeable in Cuban society was the lack of women in places of honour. They were there and part of the revolution alongside the men. But few are shown in propaganda, or on the money except for the Celia Sánchez watermark on some of the notes. It's mostly men and I find it a very macho society.

But apart from that, travelling off the beaten path in Cuba in 2017 was a real honour and a humbling experience, and I thank everyone who shared their stories with me.

Acknowledgements and Thanks

I would like to thank my friends and family – you know who you are – and the many people I have met along the way.

I would like to thank Chris Harris, my editor for his work on maps, photos and content.

I would also like to thank Mikalena, Anley, Rudy from Belgium and the many other wonderful Cubans I met.

Any further errors or omissions that remain are, of course, all mine.

APPENDIX

Some Useful Travel Information

Anley's Business Card. He is based at the Bayamo Travel Agent, "across from Viazul Terminal in Bayamo, cell (+53)52922209, bayamotravelagent@yahoo.com, www. bayamotravelagent.com" The formal address of the Bayamo Travel Agent is Carretera Central, #478. Bayamo.

LIST OF HOTELS INCLUDING GOVERNMENT HOTELS

http://cubazul.net/hotel-chains

List of Casas Particulares

http://www.casaparticular.org/

VIAZUL BUSES

You can find timetables on the Viazul website:
http://www.viazul.com/

or this website:
http://www.cuba-individual.com/e_horario.htm

MUSEUM OF THE REVOLUTION

https://en.wikipedia.org/wiki/Museum_of_the_Revolution_(Cuba)

It is possible to navigate around Cuba on http://www.maps.me

OTHER INFORMATION

USA CITIZENS TRAVELLING TO CUBA

http://observer.com/2016/12/travel-havana-cuba-americans/

HAVANA

https://www.tripadvisor.co.nz/Attractions-g147271-Activities-Havana_Ciudad_de_la_Habana_Province_Cuba.html

https://en.wikipedia.org/wiki/Havana

http://wikitravel.org/en/Havana

https://www.lonelyplanet.com/cuba/havana

http://www.planetware.com/tourist-attractions-/havana-cub-cdh-h.htm

https://www.tripadvisor.co.nz/Attractions-g147270-Activities-Cuba.html

http://www.stuff.co.nz/travel/destinations/south-america/87360816/tips-and-things-to-do-in-cuba-the-ultimate-guide-for-firsttime-visitors-to-postfidel-cub

https://placesjournal.org/article/history-of-the-present-havana/

VARADERO BEACH

https://en.wikipedia.org/wiki/Varadero

http://indianajo.com/2014/06/varadero-beach-resorts-cuba.html

https://www.google.co.nz/search?q=GOOGLE+varadero+beach&rlz=1C1PRFC_enNZ6 45NZ645&source=lnms&tbm=isch&sa=X&ved=0ahUKEwjq1Njqw8DSAhUBi5QKHV00AH cQ_AUICCgB&biw=1164&bih=586

CEINFUGOS

https://en.wikipedia.org/wiki/Cienfuegos

https://www.lonelyplanet.com/cuba/cienfuegos

http://www.cubajunky.com/cienfuegos/index.htm

http://whc.unesco.org/en/list/1202

https://www.tripadvisor.co.nz/Hotel_Review-g609122-d1911192-Reviews-Punta_La_Cueva-Cienfuegos_Cienfuegos_Province_Cuba.html

BAY OF PIGS

http://www.exploguide.com/site/museo-de-playa-giron-bay-pigs-war-museum

https://www.lonelyplanet.com/cuba/playa-giron

https://www.tripadvisor.co.nz/Hotel_Review-g2053537-d273662-Reviews-Hotel_Horizontes_Playa_Giron-Playa_Giron_Matanzas_Province_Cuba.html

https://www.tripadvisor.co.nz/Attraction_Review-g147270-d149885-Reviews-Peninsula_de_Zapata_National_Park-Cuba.html

https://www.tripadvisor.co.nz/Attraction_Review-g147270-d318777-Reviews-Alejandro_de_Humboldt_National_Park-Cuba.html

TRINIDAD

http://whc.unesco.org/en/list/460

https://en.wikipedia.org/wiki/Trinidad,_Cuba

http://www.gettingstamped.com/trinidad-cuba-travel-guide/

BAYAMO

https://www.lonelyplanet.com/cuba/bayamo

https://en.wikipedia.org/wiki/Bayamo

www.cuba-junky.com/granma/bayamo-home.htm

https://www.tripadvisor.co.nz/Tourism-g445055-Bayamo_Granma_Province_Cuba-Vacations.html

FIDEL CASTRO'S HIDEOUT AND PICO TURQUINO

www.cbc.ca/news/world/castro-mountain-hideout-video-1.3870050

https://www.wildfrontierstravel.com/en_GB/destination/cuba/what-to-do/granma/half-day-hike-to-fidel-s-hideout

https://www.tripadvisor.co.nz/ShowUserReviews-g2198405-d1809197-r123910539-Sierra_Maestra-Santiago_de_Cuba_Province_Cuba.html

https://www.lonelyplanet.com/cuba/travel-tips-and-articles/revolutionary-trails-cubas-best-hikes

http://cuba-turquino.blogspot.co.nz/

https://www.youtube.com/watch?v=WfbLV0pw91k

www.summitpost.org/pico-turquino/154032

https://en.wikipedia.org/wiki/Pico_Turquino

https://www.cubagrouptour.com/tour/cetreks.html

https://www.tripadvisor.co.nz/ShowTopic-g2198343-i9884-k4798971-Hiking_Pico_Turquino_anyone-Guantanamo_Province_Cuba.html

http://www.mountain-forecast.com/peaks/Pico-Turquino

SANTIAGO DE CUBA

https://www.tripadvisor.co.nz/Tourism-g147273-Santiago_de_Cuba_Santiago_de_Cuba_Province_Cuba-Vacations.html

https://www.tripadvisor.co.nz/Attractions-g147273-Activities-Santiago_de_Cuba_Santiago_de_Cuba_Province_Cuba.html

https://www.lonelyplanet.com/cuba/eastern-cuba/santiago-de-cuba

https://en.wikipedia.org/wiki/Santiago_de_Cuba

GUANTANAMO BAY

https://en.wikipedia.org/wiki/Guantanamo_Bay_detention_camp

https://en.wikipedia.org/wiki/Guant%C3%A1namo

https://en.wikipedia.org/wiki/Guantanamo_Bay_Naval_Base

http://www.reprieve.org.uk/guantanamo-week/

BARACOA

http://wikitravel.org/en/Baracoa

https://en.wikivoyage.org/wiki/Baracoa

http://www.baracoa.org/

https://en.wikipedia.org/wiki/Baracoa

https://www.lonelyplanet.com/cuba/eastern-cuba/baracoa

CAMAGUEY

http://whc.unesco.org/en/list/1270

http://www.lonelyplanet.com/cuba/camaguey/introduction

https://en.wikipedia.org/wiki/Camagüey

https://www.youtube.com/user/JoopSiroop

https://www.tripadvisor.co.nz/Tourism-g147272-Camaguey_Camaguey_Province_Cuba-Vacations.html

Made in the USA
Middletown, DE
24 March 2019